OMAHA STEAKS

LET'S GRILL

John Harrisson with Frederick J. Simon

Published by Clarkson Potter/Publishers,
New York, New York.
Member of the Crown Publishing Group.

Random House, Inc.
New York, Toronto, London, Sydney, Auckland
www.randomhouse.com

CLARKSON N. POTTER is a trademark and
POTTER and colophon are registered trademarks
of Random House, Inc.

Printed in China.
Library of Congress Cataloging-in-Publication
Harrisson, John.
    Omaha Steaks: Let's Grill/by John Harrisson with
    Frederick J. Simon—1st ed.
    1. Barbecue cookery. I. Simon, Frederick J. II. Title
    TX840.B3 H38 2001
    641.5'784--dc21

                                                00-039958

ISBN 0-609-60776-6
10 9 8 7 6 5 4 3 2

Contents

4

Beef

Pork

Lamb

Chicken

Seafood

Vegetables

Dessert

Foreword

In the words of the late James Beard, one of the first great cooks to fully appreciate the American grilling tradition, "What fun is there to a picnic or a barbecue if there is present the feeling of discipline or restraint? Whether your first task is to be grilling two lamb chops or barbecuing a couple of pigs...do either with heart and spirit and have a good time doing it. Otherwise there is no point to this business at all." I could not agree more.

For me, good fellowship is at the heart of this whole cooking endeavor. I remember the best meals I've ever had not only because of the food, but also because of my companions. Cracking blue crabs and drinking cans of beer at a joint on Maryland's Eastern Shore with a couple of cooking buddies, or slurping oysters, peeling shrimp, and downing margaritas in Florida with my first mentor-chef and his wife—those were truly outstanding meals. No matter how good the food, it doesn't really qualify as a great meal if nobody else is there.

This approach to cooking, eating, and life in general isn't for everybody, but for me having fun is key. And I've always felt that there's no better way of enjoying food than grilling or barbecuing. When I was a kid, my father (a classic dad griller) would come home from work in the summer and call to me on his way upstairs to change his clothes, "We're grilling tonight, get the fire ready." I would go outside, dump out the ashes, and clean the grill; Dad would come down wearing shorts. He would watch as I squeezed on twice as much lighter fluid as necessary, then he'd let me light the match and we'd both enjoy the fireball that shot up into the sky (I can say now that this approach is not to be recommended. In retrospect, I am lucky to still have hair!) When the flames died down, he and I would stand there and cook. Upon delivery of the food indoors to my mom, he would boast that we'd "done it again"—another fantastic meal from the wilds of the backyard. And each time, as he took the first bite, he would proclaim it "the best meal yet." The point of this story is to encourage you to relax—don't get too tied down or intimidated. Grilling should be approached in a laid-back, lighthearted way. The fun should be in the cooking and the eating, not in the perfection of the craft.

Grilling is the most straightforward of all cooking methods: what could be more basic than putting something over a fire and cooking until it's done? However, the constantly changing dynamic of a live fire means that grilling is also the most interactive and, therefore, by far the most exciting and challenging of all cooking methods. When you cook inside at a stove, you just turn the oven to 350°F to bake a cake, or you just twist the dial to medium-high for sautéing. But for grilling, you must make constant, intuitive decisions based on observation and experience. And since no two fires are alike, each time you approach the grill you are facing a new culinary landscape, a cooking adventure complete with the possibility of triumph or failure. This provides a uniquely exciting cooking experience—"the thrill of the grill." Rising to this challenge is the joy of grilling. No matter what you think about your cooking skills, if you're willing to spend a few short hours playing with fire in your backyard, you can become an excellent griller, which in my mind sure beats standing over a stove.

At both of my restaurants—the East Coast Grill in Cambridge, Massachusetts, and the Back Eddy, in Westport, Massachusetts—I feature live-fire grilling; I've competed in international barbecue competitions and have written several books on the subject. For me, grilling is much more than a cooking technique; it's an invitation to relax, have fun, and enjoy tasty food. When it comes right down to it, some of the best of times I've shared with good friends have been around live fires with delicious, smoky grilled food on our plates.

—Chris Schlesinger

"There is no fire without some smoke."

John Heywood, *Collected Proverbs (1.546)*

Preface

If you are an American, then you probably grew up with a father who possessed the mysterious Grilling Gene. This is the wonder of human biology that makes grown men king of the grill even if they cannot so much as boil an egg in a home kitchen. (I don't want to exclude women, but surveys show that 70 percent of all grillers and barbecuers are men.) Most of us grew up with a barbecue grill in the backyard, or at least within sniffing distance of one. Our families and friends would make a grand and even memorable event of the cookout, the centerpiece of which is the trusty grill.

We have seen an incredible growth in the number of households with a grill, as well as in restaurants that offer wood-burning grilled food. After all, grilling and barbecuing are quintessentially American—what better excuse to get together, enjoy the great outdoors, eat good, tasty food, and share spirited conversation? For some, grilled food is the ultimate comfort food, in tune with the renewed interest in home cooking over the last 20 years. Many folks appreciate that grilling is informal and unpretentious—what you see and smell is what you get. Jeans and sneakers (or sometimes boots) are standard dress code, and paper napkins are the norm. On the other hand, grilling can just as easily lend itself to elegant dinners and fine wines to match, as some of the recipes that follow prove.

Grilling skill comes with experience, but it can be gained quickly. Unlike other cooking methods that are as predictable as can be, grilling always offers something new and fun to learn. There is a sense of ceremony that harks back to our primal roots—and the smell and taste of grilled foods can't be replicated. Grilling is the only cooking method that allows an unmistakable smoky flavor, a perfectly seared crust, and the attractive crosshatch grill marks that set the mouth watering and invite the hungry to dig in.

My family business, Omaha Steaks, was founded by two men who left Riga, Latvia, in 1898 to escape religious persecution. J. J. Simon and his son, B. A., boarded a ship for the United States and a new life. After passing through Ellis Island, they got on a train going west and got off when the land looked like Riga farm country: Omaha, Nebraska, their new home. After learning American business methods, they bought a building downtown in 1917 and founded the Omaha Steaks meat business. I think it's safe to say that today they wouldn't recognize the company, which now manufactures, markets, and distributes a wide variety of gourmet foods nationwide and overseas, and employs more than 1,800 people.

I inherited a love of grilling. B. A.'s son, my late father, Lester Simon, was my first and most influential grilling teacher—he loved to grill all kinds of meats year-round. In 1954, Mom and Dad built a new home in Omaha with a charcoal grill built into the kitchen, which allowed Dad to bring his grilling indoors during our cold Nebraska winters. The joy of grilling is part of our family heritage, and I hope that this book will make it part of yours, too.

—Frederick J. Simon

"Through our great good fortune, in our youth our hearts were touched with fire."

Oliver Wendell Holmes

Introduction
History & Fundamentals

Ever since man discovered fire, we have cooked over it. No doubt our species survived the early days of deprivation and danger by means of a nicely grilled hunk of meat. We have always been hunters, scavengers, and gatherers, and whatever our station in life or kitchen comforts, many— maybe even most—of us still feel the primal urge to grill. Grilling is more popular now than ever. Some would say it is undergoing a renaissance; others, that we are witnessing a new paradigm in cooking. Whatever the case, grilling has been around for a very long time, and it is here to stay.

Technically, barbecuing and grilling are two different things, as we will explore later (see pages 12 to 13). But in practice, the terms are commonly used interchangeably, and some recipes even call for a combination of the two methods. Grilling involves cooking over high, direct heat; barbecuing is done over lower heat, often indirectly. Both techniques can be used on today's grills, using all forms of heating sources—charcoal, wood, gas, or electricity. So while the focus of this book is grilling, we also include recipes and information on barbecuing.

A Little History

Many theories exist about the origin of the word *barbecue*. One states that it is derived from the Zapotec Indians of Mexico; their word *barbacoa* refers to cooking foods slowly in a pit in the ground lined with heated stones. Another theory says that the word comes from the French *barbe à queue*, meaning "beard to tail," the way of roasting a whole animal over a fire.

How far back this technique goes is anyone's guess, but almost certainly to the Neolithic times, or the Stone Age. Centuries ago, Polynesian settlers brought barbecue to Hawaii with the *imu*, or underground oven or pit; imu-cooked pig is still the centerpiece of the Hawaiian luau. The Quechua people of Peru enjoy a similar tradition, the *pachamanca*, or "earth oven"; in Mexico's Yucatán, the oven is a *pib*, and foods cooked in it are *pibil*. In the American Northeast, early settlers copied clambakes (seafood cooked in heated pits on the beach) from native tribes, and Plains

Indians smoked meats during the summer and fall to sustain them during the harsh winters.

Like barbecuing, grilling over open flames is a universal technique with long and widespread roots. Native Americans of the Pacific Northwest secured whole salmon to cedar planks and cooked them over an open fire. In South America, *churrasquerías*—restaurants specializing in grilled meats cooked over enormous fires—can be found everywhere, a tradition popularized long ago by the *gauchos* of Argentina. Cuisines as disparate as Greek, Indian, and Japanese all enjoy a tradition of grilling over open fires—from the beach grills on the Spanish coast cooking *bocorones* (whitebait) to street braziers in Indonesia.

In the United States, the different ethnic immigrants brought grilling and barbecue traditions with them. One theory behind the importance of barbecue in Texas, for instance, is the significant numbers of German and Central European immigrants during the nineteenth century who brought traditions of sausage making and meat curing. As the Western expansion gathered pace, an enduring romantic image was pioneers cooking over an open fire underneath the stars; later, it was the cowboys of nineteenth-century cattle drives gathering around the fire, playing harmonicas. And more recently, President Lyndon Johnson's White House lawn barbecues may have contributed the most to making grilling an American institution.

So why do grilling and barbecuing remain popular? Perhaps people just enjoy socializing in a relaxed setting; or maybe the fire and smoke and grease stains bring out the macho best (or the little boy) in all of us, and provide an excuse to wear that favorite stained old apron. That it can be done almost anywhere—in a backyard, on a patio or balcony, or even at a picnic—is certainly appealing. And the techniques are simple, inexact yet challenging, and open to intuition and personal interpretation—the grilling experience is different every time. But hopefully, grilling and barbecuing endure because of the best reason of all: they're *fun*.

Fundamentals

Grilling

Grilling, the most popular method of cooking with flame or fire, is usually done over a **direct** heat source: charcoal briquettes, lump charcoal, gas, and wood are the most popular sources. Grilling particularly suits tender, relatively thin, high-quality cuts of meat (especially steaks and chops), which are best cooked over high heat (500°F or more) for a short period of time (20 minutes or less). This results in meat seared on the outside with a caramelized crust (due to the biochemistry of the process), with the internal juices sealed inside. Other quick-cooking items such as burgers, sausages, hot dogs, chicken, fish, shellfish, and vegetables are also best grilled quickly over relatively high heat.

Grilling can be done with or without the grill cover. Food will cook more quickly if covered because of the increased heat. Covering will also maximize the smoky flavor, especially if you use wood or wood chips. A covered grill needs to be vented to some extent, to prevent the fire from going out. As a general rule, grilled foods should be turned once, about halfway through the cooking process.

Barbecuing

The term *barbecue* (a.k.a. Bar-B-Q, BBQ, 'cue, or, to the real aficionados, simply Q) is often used synonymously with *grilling*. But technically, barbecue involves slow cooking with smoke over **indirect**, low heat (250°F or less)—just enough to cook the food. Traditionally, barbecuing is done in an outside underground pit, or in a purpose-built, barrel-shaped contraption with soaked wood chunks or chips. But it can also be done effectively on a covered grill.

The food is placed away from the coals, directly over a drip pan to prevent flare-ups. On a gas grill, a side burner can be used; if there are two burners, one can be left unlit and the food placed over it.

Larger or less tender cuts of meat such as roasts, loins, brisket, whole poultry and fish, spare ribs, and pork shoulder are best suited to barbecuing, as it helps break down the tough connective tissues in the meat (rather like braising). For some cuts of meat, as well as for other foods such as vegetables and fish, barbecuing is done mainly for the intense smoky flavor. For best results, a container of water should be placed in the barbecue or grill to provide some humidity, which helps prevent the meat from drying out. This said, heated debates often arise about the best techniques, sauces, and marinades, as well as other fine points of cooking with smoke.

Grill Roasting

This term describes covered grilling over direct or indirect heat at a higher temperature than barbecuing, but not as high as plain grilling (typically, 300°F to 375°F). Grill roasting works like the convection heat of an oven, but with live fire. It is best for tender, larger cuts of meat that do not need long, slow cooking, but that benefit from developing a nice crust, without burning—pork loin, whole chicken, chicken pieces, roasts, and ribs, for example. Grill roasting can impart more of a smoky flavor than grilling, but less so than barbecuing.

Smoking (or Curing)

Wood smoke is a natural preservative and flavoring agent. Smoking is done in an enclosed container over indirect heat at low temperatures (typically 70°F to 85°F for "cold" smoking, or 100°F to 200°F for "hot" smoking). Water may be used to provide moisture, although it's usually not necessary. Because of the low temperatures, smoking can take a long time—up to 10 hours, for example, for a ham or turkey. Smoking can be done in a kettle-type charcoal grill, but because the temperature is difficult to control, it is best done in a barrel-shaped home smoker (either charcoal, gas, or electric) that you can buy at specialty and camping stores (see Appendix C, page 119).

Spit Roasting (Rotisserie)

This increasingly popular method is grilling over direct heat on a rotating spike or skewer, allowing the food to baste itself. The heat source is usually to one side, although sometimes it is positioned underneath. On most modern grills or rotisseries, the spike or skewer is motorized.

> "O! for a Muse of fire, that would ascend the brightest heaven of invention!"
>
> **William Shakespeare,** *Henry V*

Where to Begin:
Grills & Grilling
Equipment

More and more, modern cooking technology allows us few excuses *not* to grill: there are outdoor gas and charcoal grills in every price range, from basic to sophisticated, from small and portable to large and stationary, open or covered, for indoors and out, with direct heat or both direct and indirect heat. Ever more high-tech models are developed, and many a new home now comes with an indoor vented grill or rotisserie. We are even seeing a renaissance in spit-cooking fireplaces.

We recommend opting for a well-made, sturdy grill that will last longer than one or two seasons. The cooking surface should be large enough to grill several portions of food and to provide areas of both direct and indirect heat. For gas grills, two burners are ideal, allowing for both direct and indirect cooking, and with a covered grill you can grill-roast, barbecue, and smoke-roast as well as grill. Apart from outdoor wood-burning grills and barbecues—both of which are ambitious setups that are well beyond the needs of most home cooks—grills come in three types: gas, charcoal, and electric. (For a discussion of fuel and flavorings, see page 24.) In general, most professional cooks prefer grilling over wood or charcoal, which burn hotter and yield more flavor than gas or electricity, and many home cooks would add that working with real fire is a lot more fun. But gas grilling is becoming increasingly popular because of convenience.

Gas Grills

Most gas grills are fueled by a tank of liquid propane (some hook up to a natural gas line) and use lava rock or ceramic briquettes set over burners. The price of a good-quality model starts at around $150—which is significantly more expensive than a charcoal grill—and goes up to several thousand dollars for a really sophisticated model. But gas grills are economical on fuel, easy to start, they heat up instantly, they're clean (no messy charcoal to deal with), and their heat is easier to control and maintain than charcoal. Many gas grills have side burners, which can be a real bonus for heating sauces and fixins. On the other hand, gas grills never get as hot as charcoal: a gas grill set at high will be approximately as hot as a charcoal grill at medium to medium-high heat, so grilling takes longer. Most experts also agree that the flavor gas grills give to food is less intense and complex than charcoal imparts. On the other hand, gas grills can also be installed indoors if properly connected to a natural gas source and vented.

Charcoal Grills

Many grill experts feel that the flavor of foods cooked over a charcoal fire—the most popular type of backyard grill—is superior to gas, and also provides all the thrill and fun of cooking with live fire. Because charcoal grills cook at a higher temperature than gas grills, they sear and brown meat more effectively, giving a more crusty, textured surface. Charcoal grills can be inexpensive, starting at around $35, with the more sophisticated models running into hundreds of dollars. On the down side, they take longer to prepare and heat up than gas grills, they are messier, and their heat level is more difficult to control and change.

The single most popular type of backyard charcoal grill is the Weber-style kettle, invented in the United States in the 1950s. It is usually three-legged and round, with vents above and below the grilling rack that allow temperature control: the more open, the hotter the fire. Charcoal grills provide a choice of cooking methods: grilling, grill-roasting (if a lid is used), and barbecuing (if covered) with indirect low heat and perhaps soaked wood chips or chunks. If grill-roasting or barbecuing, a drip pan should be used directly beneath the food so that fat drips into it and not onto the coals or the flame, which might cause flare-ups or grease fires. The drippings can then be used to baste the meat.

Whatever the shape of the grill (some new types are square or rectangular), the main considerations are a large cooking area and enough space for a hot fire. Grills with deep bowls are better because they allow air to circulate around the fire. A tall dome lid gives plenty of space for large pieces of meat such as roasts and whole birds. However, for some purposes—such as picnics, beach grills, or tailgating parties—the most convenient type of grill is the small, portable, open-brazier or hibachi charcoal grill. As the name suggests, hibachis originated in Japan, and they are the most reasonably priced, starting at $20. They usually have no lid, but if all you need is to grill small portions quickly, they are fuel- and time-efficient. Finally, you can also find charcoal ovens with closeable lids, which use indirect heat to cook more like an oven than a grill, but they also use smoke to flavor food. These tend to be relatively expensive.

Avoid covering a charcoal grill if possible, unless grill-roasting or barbecuing larger pieces of meat. Smoke, soot, and grease residue that accumulate on the lid over time can give the food an inferior flavor. Instead, cover food with foil or disposable metal (aluminum) cooking pans that act like mini-ovens in retaining heat.

Electric Grills

Electric grills require an electric outlet, so they are limited in terms of placement. But because there is no charcoal (and therefore no ash), they are clean, and they don't need refillable gas canisters. However, purists will tell you that electric grilling lacks the flavor, excitement, and challenge of cooking over real fire. Increasingly, specially vented flattop gas-fired and range-top electric grills can be found in new houses and apartments, and these are ideal for those who like clean grilling.

Rotisseries

Indoor or outdoor motorized rotisseries provide slow, even cooking over medium heat and do the work of turning the food. Some pricier gas grills have rotisseries built in, but they can also be bought as an extra attachment, preferably with adjustable speeds. Rotisseries work especially well for whole birds or whole firm-fleshed fish such as salmon, striped bass, or cod, and for large roasts such as legs or racks of lamb and slabs of spare ribs, which otherwise would be difficult to cook evenly on the grill. The self-basting action results in succulent, tender meat and a crispy exterior. It's important to place a drip pan beneath the meat as it cooks and to baste the meat frequently with the drippings. Make sure you thread the food so it is balanced, even if this means the meat is at an angle. The spit should turn evenly and the meat should cook evenly without moving on the spit.

Accessories

The good news is that there are seemingly endless accessories available for your grill. The bad news is that your head will spin with all the choices. You can use as many or as few accessories as your budget and inclination dictate. You really don't need much, but you can get fancy if you wish. Below are our recommendations on accessories, beginning with the most important. Some are available in supermarkets, and all can be bought at kitchen stores or restaurant-supply companies. For a discussion of accessories for lighting and maintaining charcoal fires (such as a metal chimney flue, fire starters, and wood chips), see page 26 to 27.

The Basic Tool Set

Tongs

Long-handled (at least 15 inches), heavy-duty, and prefer-ably spring-loaded tongs with a nonconductive wooden or rubber grip. Tongs allow for maneuvering and turning the food without piercing it and letting the juices escape.

Spatula

A long-handled (at least 15 inches), heavy-duty, extra-wide stainless steel spatula with a nonconductive wooden or rubber grip. Never use a plastic or nonstick spatula, which will melt or burn on the grill (or worse, on the food). Some recommend an "offset" metal spatula, where the handle is kinked downward so the scoop part is lower than the handle.

Knives

One or two good carving knives or chef's knives, items sometimes overlooked by the casual griller.

Fork

A long-handled fork (at least 15 inches long). Use the fork for lifting large pieces of meat (such as roasts and whole birds), as well as for testing doneness at the end (although the "finger test," Appendix B, page 115, is preferred).

Mitts

One or two thick, padded, insulated, and flame-retardant grilling (or oven) mitts that reach to the elbow.

Brush

A good-quality basting/glazing brush with natural (not nylon or artificial) pliable bristles. A 1-inch paintbrush works well, and the longer the handle, the better. Alternatively, or in addition, you can use a "mop baster," which looks like a mini-mop. Both tools can also be used to oil the grill before cooking.

Cleaning Brush

A long-handled stiff wire brush (preferably brass, which is rust-resistant), ideally with a scraper on the end to help remove hardened grease. Best used after the grill has cooled down a bit but while it is still warm, as the residue will come off much more easily than if the grill is cold.

Timer

A kitchen timer or clip-on timer to remind you to turn or remove the food.

Other Accessories

Skewers

Long metal skewers, for kabobs and satays. Flat skewers are better than round ones because the food is less likely to spin around when turned. (To solve this problem, use two skewers parallel to each other, or a two-pronged skewer, available at good kitchen stores). Long bamboo skewers should be soaked in water for at least 30 minutes before grilling so the exposed parts don't burn, and they should be positioned with the exposed ends over the coolest part of the fire. Always use an oven mitt to handle any type of skewers.

Thermometer

A stainless steel meat thermometer with circular dial, for larger pieces of meat. Since this must be inserted at least 2 inches into the food, it is also helpful to have an instant–read thermometer for steaks and other thin cuts. Keep checking the internal temperature of the meat if you want it cooked to the right degree of doneness, and never leave a thermometer in the meat while grilling.

Grill Temperature Gauge

Insert through a vent hole in the lid to check temperature, although most gas grills have one built in.

Baskets

Long-handled, wire-mesh, hinged grill baskets, for grilling whole fish, sliced vegetables, small items that might otherwise fall through the cooking grid, and even burgers and chicken breasts. A variation on this theme is a wire vegetable rack that attaches to the inside edge of the grill. Because the heat is lower at the edge of the grill, the vegetables held by the wire rack will cook more slowly and acquire a smokier flavor when grilling larger pieces of food in the center of the grill. Roast holders and rib racks are also available for standing roasts and ribs off the cooking grate.

Spray Bottle of Water

Invaluable for flare-ups or just for cooling the fire. (But don't overdo it!)

Kitchen Cloths

Wet wipes or kitchen cloths that you don't care about too strongly, for wiping tools and hands.

Pans

A supply of disposable (but reusable) aluminum pans of various sizes for use as drip trays and for transporting meat and ingredients to and from the grill. These can also be used for soaking wood chips and to hold marinades or water when you are cooking over indirect heat and want moisture inside the grill to prevent foods from drying out.

Cover

A plastic or fabric cover, to protect the grill from the elements. Place over the grill only after it is completely cool.

Table

A portable side table is invaluable for tools, plates, and ingredients. Most newer gas and large charcoal grills have built-in tables, but kettle grills, for example, do not.

> "The fire which seems extinguished often slumbers beneath the ashes."
>
> Pierre Corneille *(seventeenth century)*

Where and Why: Location & Safety Issues

Siting Your Grill

Here are some issues to consider when deciding where you should place your grill:

- Place the grill on a level surface and make sure it is well ventilated.

- Unless you have a properly vented electric or gas grill, never grill indoors, in a garage, or in any other enclosed area, as it creates a potential fire hazard. It may also cause potentially lethal carbon monoxide fumes and breathing problems associated with smoke in an enclosed space—not to mention potential smoke damage to your home.

- Keep the grill away from anything combustible such as leaves, trees, fences, buildings, awnings, eaves, and vehicles. Keep the grill several feet away from walls, deck railings, utility poles, and so on.

- If at all possible, put the grill where you feel comfortable and have a view. Remember, grilling should be an enjoyable and sociable activity.

- If there is any chance of rain or a very hot sun, make sure that both you and the grill are sheltered.

- Place the grill within easy reach of the kitchen, for accessibility to ingredients and serving supplies, while still being close to your supply of charcoal and wood.

- If you are grilling at dusk or after dark, site the grill within reach of outdoor lights, or at least have a powerful flashlight.

- If you are grilling or barbecuing for any extended time, have a comfortable chair—grilling is much more fun when you see it as an opportunity to commune with the fire and relax.

Safe Grilling

Once you have located your grill, bear several safety measures in mind:

- Take your time. If you feel pressed and pressured, it's probably not a good idea to grill.

- Expect to experiment with cooking times and grilling techniques, and allow time for it. Wind and cold will lower the grill temperature and increase the cooking time.

- Before using a grill for first time, thoroughly and carefully read the manufacturer's instructions, paying special attention to warning labels and safety information.

- Keep the fire under control at all times, especially when lighting charcoal with lighter fluid.

- When grilling with charcoal, use the proper lighter fluid. Never use gasoline, alcohol, kerosene, or any other substance, as they are volatile and can easily cause burns or even explode. Do not add lighter fuel or anything else to hot (or even warm) charcoals, especially if you value your hair, eyebrows, and clothing.

- Do not leave a grill unattended. Fire is particularly dangerous for children and pets, so keep them a safe distance away.

- Avoid grilling over charcoal when it is windy. Sparks and embers can fly, especially if you are using lump charcoal, and flames are always potentially dangerous in wind.

- Trim most fat from meat—leave no more than a quarter inch. Fat dripping onto hot coals can cause flare-ups. Aim to sear and brown meat, not scorch or blacken it.

- Before cooking, keep the grill lightly oiled to prevent foods from sticking, especially for lean foods such as fish or vegetables. Use cooking oil and a cloth, or nonstick cooking spray. Do not oil the grill once the fire is started. Alternatively, lightly brush oil on the food before placing it on the grill.

- Good organization before you begin cooking is a secret to successful grilling. Prepare what cooking professionals call the *mise en place*, where all the necessary ingredients, seasonings, and tools are prepped and ready for use. Grilling happens quickly, and planning can make a big difference between cooked and burned—and between safety and danger.

- To prevent kabobs or other types of skewered meat from sticking to the grill, place two fire-resistant bricks on either side of the center of the grill. Rest the ends of the skewers on the bricks and turn frequently.

- Take care when opening the cover of a grill, barbecue, or other covered container, as steam and smoke can cause injuries. Open with an oven mitt or pot holder to avoid burns. Even better, keep some thick gardening gloves close by to handle anything really hot (such as the cooking grate, coals, or ingredients).

- Avoid drinking and grilling. Most grilling burns are sustained because of carelessness caused by drinking.

- Be sure to extinguish or turn off the grill after use. For charcoal fires, the most effective method is to close all the vents and to cover the grill tightly with the lid. Do not remove any coals until they are completely cold.

- When using a gas grill for the first time in the spring or summer, check the equipment thoroughly, especially the connections and hoses from the gas supply.

- After using a gas grill, turn off the burners and turn off the gas canister or the natural-gas supply. When you turn them back on next time, if you smell gas, do not light the grill. Light a gas grill with the cover up and the burners turned to ignition setting or to high. If the grill still does not light, wait 2 or 3 minutes before trying again to allow the gas to dissipate.

- Never use old or rusty propane containers.

- For charcoal grills, keep a dry-spray extinguisher, garden hose, spray bottle of water, bucket of sand, or at least a bowl of water on hand in case of serious flare-ups. For gas grills, be prepared to turn off the gas supply.

- Store gas tanks in an open but shady outside space. Never keep them in an enclosed area such as a garage or in your house in case of leakage or explosion. Keep upright.

- Always clean your grill after you've used it or it will begin to corrode. Empty ashes when cool (old ash blocks air vents). Use a wire brush and soapy water to clean the fire and cooking grates, then wipe or spray with a little cooking oil to prevent corrosion.

Food Safety

- Although it's ideal to cook foods that have been brought to room temperature (the grill heat can penetrate and cook the center without burning the exterior), be cautious. Seafood, fish, and other thin or highly perishable foods should be refrigerated until cooked, and if it's hot outside, let meat sit just a few minutes. Never let meat sit for longer than necessary; 20 to 30 minutes from the refrigerator should get it to room temperature.

- All meats and fish should be refrigerated as soon as possible after purchase, and placed in a sealed storage bag or container on a lower shelf to prevent leakages and drips. Cook as soon as possible; freeze meat and fish if you will not be cooking it within 2 or 3 days.

- If using meat or fish that has been frozen, or if you choose to buy vacuum-sealed portions of beef that have been shipped with dry ice or a freezer pack, be sure to thaw in the refrigerator in the sealed package. This gives juicier and more flavorful results. Do not thaw meat or fish at room temperature; if you need to take a short-cut, thaw sealed packages of meat or fish in cold water; using a microwave is the least recommended. Meat can be refrozen if it has been thawed in the refrigerator for a day or two and either still contains ice crystals or is still cold to the touch (at or below 40°F). Seal the meat or fish tightly in freezer bags with as little air inside as possible, and use within 2 or 3 months for best results.

- Rinse off poultry and fish before cooking. For handling meat and fish safely, never use the same cutting board, work surface, bowl, plate, or platter for raw and cooked ingredients. Thoroughly wash hands, utensils, cutting boards, and work surfaces that come into contact with raw food with warm, soapy water.

- Do not use marinades in which meat or fish have sat unless you boil them for at least 3 or 4 minutes.

- Cook meat and fish to the desired doneness; do not par-grill and reserve.

- Once cooked, do not let meat or fish sit at room temperature for more than a few minutes, and refrigerate leftovers immediately.

"For violent fires soon burn out themselves; Small showers last long but sudden storms are short."

William Shakespeare, *Richard I.*

Firing Up the Grill:
Fuel & Flavorings

Wood

Whether you are lucky enough to own a wood-burning grill or plan on using chunks or chips, nothing beats the original grill fuel for giving an authentic, deliciously smoky flavor. On the other hand, wood is more unpredictable than charcoal or gas, and you need time to prepare a wood fire, as well as storage space for the wood, preferably under cover.

Fruit woods (apple, cherry, and peach) and nut woods (hickory, pecan, and almond) are best for grilling. Mesquite is also popular for flavor, and it burns hotter and longer than most, but it throws out showers of sparks, so it needs careful attention. Maple, oak, and even grapevines are also used, while salmon aficionados will suggest alder. All these woods burn evenly and at a suitably high temperature, and they burn quickly enough to give a bed of hot coals that is perfect for grilling. None of them is *too* smoky, and they all impart rich tastes. Their flavor differences are subtle, so experiment for the best combination. We recommend nut woods and mesquite for beef and lamb, fruit woods and maple for poultry and fish, and hickory, pecan, maple, and oak for pork.

All woods should be aged at least a year or they will be too resinous, smoky, and "green." Split the wood into lengths about 1 foot long and not too thick (an inch or so). Use newspaper and kindling to get started; it is ready for cooking when the fire is reduced to glowing embers. In addition to locating a good source of already-aged wood, you might approach fruit or nut orchard owners and ask to collect their prunings, which you can age at home. Evergreen woods such as pine or fir are too resinous and burn unevenly, so are unsuitable for grilling. Never grill with any kind of treated wood, including plywood, which contains dangerous chemicals.

You don't need a wood-burning grill to replicate the unique flavor of wood. The easiest alternatives to whole branches or twigs are aromatic **wood chips** or **chunks** (such as apple, hickory, or mesquite) to a charcoal fire, or to add wood chips to a smoker box for gas. Soak the wood in water for at least a half hour before adding to the grill. If you do not have a smoker box, you can wrap the wood in heavy-duty foil, poke some small holes in it to allow the chips to smolder and smoke, and place the packet directly over the burners.

Do not add so much wood at once that it drastically lowers the heat or puts out the fire—let the wood smolder gradually. Wood chips work best for covered grill-roasting or barbecuing; they tend to burn too fast for grilling.

For extra flavor, consider adding soaked bunches of fresh or dried herbs onto the grill fire or in the smoker box. Rosemary sprigs, for example, are ideal for lamb; thyme and sage work well with pork. Bay leaves, cinnamon sticks, and star anise are other flavorings worth experimenting with.

Charcoal

Charcoal is cleaner, hotter, and more fuel-efficient than fresh or aged wood, burns hotter than gas, and contributes more flavor than gas grilling. Charcoal will burn for 30 to 45 minutes once the fire is ready for grilling before it needs replenishing. There are two forms of charcoal for grilling:

Natural Lump Charcoal

Also called "charwood," this is made from mesquite, oak, hickory, or other hardwood that is kiln-fired at very high temperatures with no additives, so the result is all-natural pure carbon. Completely dry and light in weight, lump charcoal is shaped irregularly, unlike compact briquettes. Natural lump charcoal starts quicker and burns faster and hotter (and is more expensive) than briquettes, which makes it particularly good for searing meats. Many experts will tell you that it also smells cleaner, although this is debatable.

Charcoal Briquettes

Made with ground and compressed charcoal, starch, and coal dust, briquettes are sold in bags ranging from 5 to 50 pounds. We recommend high-quality brands, which will not burn as quickly as budget brands. Briquettes burn longer and more evenly than lump charcoal, which makes them ideal for indirect grilling. Even if they provide slightly less flavor, as some maintain, briquettes can be used with soaked wood chips to give plenty of smoky tones. Once lit, a briquette fire takes 25 to 30 minutes to be ready for grilling. Some briquettes are available with firestarter added, obviating the need for liquid starter; these burn more quickly so should be mixed with plain briquettes. The cleanest option of all is ready-to-go briquettes in a bag—you just light the bag! But note that ceramic briquettes or lava rocks are only for gas grills.

Building the Charcoal Fire

We recommend preparing a fire with more than one heat level—direct heat for searing and indirect heat for longer, slower cooking. This involves building a single layer of charcoal and then adding another layer over half of the area. However, if you are simply grilling steak of uniform thickness, one even layer should suffice. In either case, be generous with the amount of fuel: it is easier to control and lower the temperature of a hot fire, if necessary, than to revive a cool one. If you prepare a single level, place thicker cuts of meat or vegetables on the hottest part of the grill (usually at the center), and put thinner ones at the edges. As you cook, shift the cooked pieces to the edges until all ingredients are evenly cooked. The same kind of maneuvering can be done with more than one level of heat.

Arrange the charcoal in an area 2 or 3 square inches larger than the food to be cooked, but leave space at the edge of the grill where you can keep ingredients warm without them cooking any longer. If you have an adjustable fire grate, place it 4 or 5 inches below the cooking grate, or vice versa. This will ensure even medium to medium-high heat. For cooking over high heat, add another layer of charcoal, or reduce the distance between the fire grate and cooking grate to 2 or 3 inches.

Lighting the Charcoal Fire

Whichever type of charcoal you use, the most efficient lighting is with a **metal chimney** or **flue starter**: a metal cylindrical container about 6 inches across, with air vents at the bottom and a wooden or heatproof handle that holds up to 2 pounds of charcoal. Chimneys are inexpensive and available at hardware or cooking stores. With a metal chimney you don't need lighter fluid, which some folks are convinced affects flavor (although it should have long since burned off before grilling). Even without lighter fuel, briquettes contain chemicals that must be burned off before you can cook over them. (This is not an issue for lump charcoal.) To use, place some crumpled newspaper in the bottom, add a little kindling if desired (but not necessary), and fill with charcoal. Place the chimney in the center of the fire grate and open the vents. Light the paper and the charcoal will begin to burn. After 15 to 20 minutes, when the charcoal is glowing, use a mitt to handle the flue, and release the coals onto the grate. Add more charcoal as necessary and wait until the coals are just covered with gray ash. If you need to add more charcoal, set the chimney on a fireproof surface and light more charcoal in it, then add to the fire grate as before.

Alternatively for charcoal, use lighter fluid. Squirt up to $1/2$ cup onto the charcoal, wait a minute or two to let it absorb the fluid, then repeat. Light carefully, keep the grill uncovered, and wait until the charcoal is covered with gray ash, 25 to 30 minutes, which is plenty of time for the fluid to burn off and evaporate (see page 21 to 23 for safety issues). Another method of lighting charcoal is old-fashioned wood kindling: place commercial kindling, dry twigs, or small pieces of wood on the fire grate over crumpled newspaper set beneath the grate. Place the charcoal over the kindling and light the newspaper.

Some folks favor the electric coil starter: a metal coil with a plastic handle that you place on the cooking grate, under the charcoal. Just plug into a grounded electric outlet (most coil leads are only a few feet long, so you may need a heavy-duty extension cord), and the red-hot coil ignites the charcoal after 5 to 10 minutes. Unplug and remove the coil gently, taking great care of both the hot coil and the charcoal; use long-handled tongs to reorganize the coals. Let the coil cool off in a safe place on a fireproof surface. Don't leave the coil under the coals too long or it will burn out. An electric coil starter costs around $10 at hardware stores.

Other satisfactory starters include compressed fuel-treated wood and chemical mixtures such as blocks of solid paraffin starter; once these burn off, there is no odor. Be sure to follow the packaging instructions.

Maintaining the Charcoal Fire

A charcoal fire is ready when the charcoal is uniformly covered with gray ash, typically 25 to 30 minutes after lighting. If it's dark outside, you can tell the fire is ready when the coals glow red, with no flames. Test by spreading out the coals with tongs, putting the cooking grate in place, covering the grill, and letting it warm for 5 minutes. Then place your hand 4 or 5 inches above the grate: you should be able to hold it there 5 seconds for a medium fire, or 2 seconds for a hot fire (4 seconds for medium-hot, 6 or 7 seconds for low). If you need a hotter fire, lower the cooking grid, open the vents, add more charcoal, or gently tap the grill or the coals with tongs to remove some of the ash. If the fire is too hot, raise the cooking grid, spread out the coals, open the lid, or close the vents somewhat.

Gas

Gas grills light simply and cleanly, and once they are heated—10 minutes covered (compared to 25 to 30 minutes for charcoal)—they are ready for grilling. You never need to add charcoal, and it is easy to control the heat at the turn of a dial. But unless you add wood chips to the smoker box or make a foil package (see page 24 to 25), gas grills cannot replicate the smokiness of charcoal; on the other hand, this tends to leave meats juicier as smoke dehydrates foods. You might consider buying mesquite-flavored ceramic briquettes, which gradually release their aroma as they burn down.

Notes on
Ingredients,
Storage, & Handling

General Notes

You should always use top-quality ingredients. Grilling is an uncomplicated technique with little mystery attached. What you see is pretty much what you get, so you'll want the ingredients to be at their best to showcase your talents. Remember, average-quality ingredients will give you only average results.

Portions

Typical portion size for main-course meat dishes is 5 to 8 ounces. Most of the recipes in this book fall within this range, and the exceptions (16-ounce porterhouse and T-bone steaks, for example) are a function of the size of cut. By all means choose smaller cuts if you are concerned about diet, appetite, or cost, and make adjustments to the recipes as necessary.

Cuts of Meat

In general, thicker cuts of meat (1 inch or more) grill better than thinner ones, as the juices do not dry out. Note that bone-in cuts take longer than boneless ones.

Heat

For beginners, practice your art over medium to medium-high heat, rather than high. This way, you will become acquainted with timing and doneness with less risk of burning the ingredients.

Marinades

A majority of the recipes in this book involve marinating meat or applying a dry rub, which may seem sacrilegious to some. In truth, many tender cuts need little or no embellishment and can be prepared with a light brushing of oil (if that), sprinkled with salt and pepper, and then the grill will weave its magic. By all means feel free to take this approach. But for maximizing flavor and texture, and for infusing meat with a touch of the exotic now and then, we recommend a little embellishment. And many cuts used in this book, such as ribs and kebabs, *need* rubs, marinades, or glazes for best results.

Marinades add moisture and flavor, very important factors for grilling. Marinate in nonreactive bowls or containers (such as stainless steel, ceramic, or glass) and always marinate meat in the refrigerator. Do not use leftover marinade as a sauce unless you boil it for a few minutes to kill any bacteria from the raw food. If you do cook marinades, they usually make delicious sauces.

Fat

A little fat can be a wonderful thing. The most flavorful cuts of meat contain some fat, and this helps the meat retain its moisture and juiciness. Of course, this does not mean you have to *eat* all of the fat, but as with most things in life, taken in moderation, some fat is okay with us.

Beef

- The most important contributor to flavor in beef, as in other meats, is the internal fat, or "marbling." Some people assume that the leaner the meat, the more tender it is likely to be, but the opposite is true. As the meat cooks, the fat melts and surrounds the fiber cells, holding in water-soluble proteins that are high in aroma and flavor as well as in valuable nutrients. Marbling should be white in color, not yellow, and it should run throughout the meat.

- The best bets when it comes to grilling are filet mignon, top sirloin, boneless strip, porterhouse, T-bone, and rib-eye (filet of prime rib). These cuts can be grilled plain with excellent results, but in most of the following recipes we use rubs and marinades to accentuate flavor. Skirt steak and flank steak are less tender but also take well to the grill.

- Look for USDA-graded beef, the standardized yardstick of quality. *Prime* and *Choice* contain more marbling and therefore tend to be juicier, more tender, and more flavorful than other cuts. *Choice*, a little less tender and flavorful than *Prime*, is the most common grade of all. *Select* (formerly *Good*) is still a superior grade, falling below the quality of *Choice*, which describes leaner cuts with relatively little marbling.

- For best results, sear beef (especially larger cuts) over high heat before cooking over lower heat. Searing helps seal in the juices. We recommend cooking steaks no more than medium; beyond that, they will dry out and become tough.

- Aging beef for at least seven days (and up to twenty-one) improves the flavor because the natural enzymes in the beef break down the fibers of the meat. If you are seeking a steak with great flavor, track down aged beef.

Pork

- These days, pork is bred lean, and cuts such as chops, cutlets, and loin—among the favorites for grilling—are low in fat.

- When buying chops, look for firm, white to pale pink meat, without marbling. With other cuts of pork, some marbling is fine, but if the meat or fat is yellow, do not buy it.

- Pork butt (cut from the shoulder) is favored for barbecuing because of the fat content, which keeps meat moist during the long cooking process.

- There are three main types of pork ribs: baby back, spareribs, and country-style. Baby backs, cut from the loin or back, are small, meaty, and tender. The larger spareribs, cut from the underside (lower rib cage), are less meaty but particularly flavorful; they are the most popular type of pork rib. If the skirt—a flap of meat—is attached to the slab of ribs, they are called Kansas City–style; if the skirt is cut off, they are known as St. Louis–style. Meaty country-style ribs, cut from the rib end of the loin, only contain small bones but are fattier and less tender, and so are less favored for grilling.

- Pork (like poultry) should be grilled over medium or medium-high heat only (not high) as it must be cooked through, to around 160°F. You can sear it first over higher heat and then move it to a medium or medium-high heat. However, overcooked pork will be dry and tough.

- Pork is done when the required internal temperature is reached, the juices run clear, and there is no pink meat near the bone. For those concerned about the trichinosis parasite, which is now believed to have been virtually eradicated in pigs raised commercially in the United States, it is killed when the internal temperature reaches around 140°F, well below the recommended 160°F required for doneness.

Lamb

- Lamb is probably the most popular grilling meat in the world, even if it is often overlooked in the United States.

- Among the most favored cuts for grilling are whole racks, rib chops, loins, loin chops, legs, and leg steaks. Increasingly, lamb is being enjoyed cooked medium-rare to medium, as with beef.

- Many people have a bias against lamb because they think the flavor is "gamey." While this was often true of mutton (meat from older sheep), improvements in breeding and the predominance of younger, leaner animals on the market nowadays make this a nonissue. By definition, lamb is less than a year old, and it is often just a few months old.

- Like beef, and unlike other types of meat, lamb is USDA-graded. The two superior grades are *Prime* and *Choice*, with the latter the most widely available.

- Look for lamb that has light red meat—lighter in color than beef. The fat around the meat should be white and a little soft to the touch, not hard.

Poultry

- If at all possible, buy fresh chickens rather than frozen. Avoid buying chickens that have bruised or blotchy skins.

- We recommend free-range, hormone- and antibiotic-free chickens, which can be purchased from health-food stores. They may be more expensive, but they are more flavorful and more healthful.

- If the skin of the chicken feels slimy, or if the uncooked chicken meat has an unusual or strange aroma, do not cook or eat it.

- Chicken skin is remarkably nonporous, so when using marinades, remove the skin. Rubs, on the other hand, can be applied on the skin, making it both flavorful and crispy, or they can be applied beneath the skin once it has been loosened with your fingertips. Of course, rubs can also be applied to skinless chicken.

- When preparing whole chicken, be sure to remove the giblets and rinse the bird under cold running water, inside and out, then pat dry with paper towels.

- Poultry (like pork) should be grilled over medium or medium-high heat only (not high) as it must be cooked through to 175°F (or 180°F for whole birds) in order to eliminate salmonella and other harmful bacteria. The exception to this rule is duck breast, which can safely be grilled to medium-rare, if desired.

- For chicken and duck, we recommend grilling skin-side down to begin. White chicken meat cooks more quickly than dark, so if cooking different chicken parts at the same time, watch closely for doneness.

Fish and Seafood

- Use only the freshest fish and shellfish. If there is a "fishy" or an ammonia-type aroma, do not buy or cook it. Fresh fish will have a clean, fresh smell, bright and shiny eyes (not clouded), red gills, and smooth, glossy skin.

- Grilling whole fish on the bone, like roasting, is the best method of preserving all the delicate juices and flavors of moist fish.

- In general, whole fish and moist or oily firm-fleshed fish such as tuna, salmon, swordfish, halibut, snapper, trout, and mahimahi are best for grilling. Delicate fish such as sole are not well-suited as they are likely to break up on the grill, and their subtle flavor may be compromised.

- Be sure to oil the cooking grate and to make sure the grate is hot before adding fish, to prevent it from sticking to the grill.

- There is a fine line between undercooking fish and overcooking it. Most white-fleshed fish need to be cooked just through or it will feel rubbery; if cooked too much, it will be dry and some of the flavor will have evaporated. There are some exceptions: many people enjoy sushi-quality tuna cooked rare or medium-rare, and many prefer salmon medium-rare to medium, for example.

Seasonings and Spices

- For ground spices, freshly grind whole seeds yourself, preferably after toasting them, for maximum intensity. Toasting brings out all the complex, intense flavors of spices by activating their essential oils. Place the whole seeds (such as cumin) in a dry skillet over low heat and toast for 1 minute, or until fragrant, stirring or tossing continuously. Take care not to scorch or the spices will taste bitter.

- Use freshly cracked or ground pepper, and kosher or sea salt rather than table salt.

The bite comes from canned chipotle chiles (dried smoked jalapeños), which are available from Latin markets. To avoid the heat, substitute 1/2 cup mild prepared salsa; you can also substitute grated Monterey Jack for the goat cheese.

Grilled Sweet
Corn Soup
(That Bites!)

Grill the bell peppers over direct medium-high heat, remove, and let steam (see page 113 to 114). When cool, peel, seed, and julienne the peppers. Set aside. While the peppers are cooling, brush the corn with the oil and grill over indirect medium heat for about 15 minutes, turning frequently, until lightly browned on all sides. Remove and, when cool enough to handle, cut the kernels from the cobs and transfer two-thirds of the corn to a blender. Add the stock and blend until smooth. Transfer to a saucepan and heat over medium-high heat.

Meanwhile, cook the bacon in a dry skillet over medium heat until cooked through, about 5 minutes. Drain on paper towels, dice, and add to the saucepan. In the rendered bacon fat, sauté the onion and garlic for 5 minutes. Transfer to the saucepan together with the cream, chipotle purée, the reserved corn, and the julienned roasted peppers. Heat until warmed through and season with salt and pepper. Ladle into serving bowls and sprinkle the marjoram and cheese over the top.

SERVES: 4

2 red bell peppers

4 ears fresh sweet corn, husked

2 teaspoons olive oil

4 cups chicken stock

4 slices bacon

1 onion, minced

2 cloves garlic, minced

1/2 cup heavy cream

1 tablespoon puréed canned chipotle chiles in adobo sauce, or to taste

Salt and freshly ground black pepper to taste

1 tablespoon chopped fresh marjoram leaves

3 ounces goat cheese, crumbled

Grill a whole head of garlic while you grill the
tomatoes—it's energy-efficient and will provide
valuable leftovers. Grilling tomatoes brings out their
complex deeper flavors, and this combination of
tomatoes, basil, and balsamic vinegar is a classic.

Charred Tomato &
Garlic Soup
with Balsamic Vinegar

2 pounds plum tomatoes

2 tablespoons olive oil

1 onion, diced

1 shallot, minced

1 tablespoon tomato
paste

1/2 teaspoon sugar

2 cloves grilled garlic
(page 113)

2 cups chicken stock

1/4 cup heavy cream

Salt and freshly ground
black pepper to taste

4 teaspoons aged
balsamic vinegar

1 1/2 tablespoons minced
fresh basil leaves

Grill the tomatoes over indirect
medium-high heat, turning often,
until the skins are somewhat
cracked and partly blackened,
about 15 minutes. (Do not overcook
or they will taste bitter.) Remove
and, when cool enough, core and
seed. (Do not worry if not all the
seeds are removed.) Transfer to a
food processor.

Heat the oil in a sauté pan and
sauté the onion and shallot over
medium-high heat for about 5 minutes, or until completely soft and
golden brown. Add the tomato
paste and sugar, and stir. Transfer
to the food processor; add the garlic, and purée until smooth. Strain
into a clean saucepan and add the
stock and cream. Season with salt
and plenty of pepper, and warm
through. Transfer to serving bowls,
drizzle or swirl 1 teaspoon of the
vinegar in the center of each serving, and garnish with the basil.
SERVES: 4

This is an ideal soup for fall when both pumpkins and fresh apples are in season. The spices echo the seasonal flavors of pumpkin pie but without the sweetness. If the weather is not conducive to grilling, broil the pumpkin instead.

Spiced Jack-o'-Lantern Soup
with Green Apple Garnish

2 pounds pumpkin flesh

2 tablespoons butter, melted, plus ¼ cup butter

1 onion, diced

1 stalk celery, sliced

1 carrot, sliced

½ teaspoon ground cinnamon

Pinch of ground nutmeg

⅛ teaspoon ground allspice

Pinch of ground cloves

Pinch of cayenne

2 teaspoons peeled and minced fresh ginger

4 cups vegetable or chicken stock

Salt and freshly ground black pepper to taste

½ cup half-and-half

1 large green apple, peeled, cored, and finely diced

Roughly chop the pumpkin flesh and brush with 1 tablespoon of the melted butter. Add some soaked wood chips to the fire and grill over direct medium-low heat for about 5 or 6 minutes per side, until tender and seared, brushing with the remaining tablespoon of melted butter. Remove and transfer to a food processor.

Heat the remaining ¼ cup of butter in a saucepan and add the onion, celery, and carrot. Sauté over medium heat for 7 to 8 minutes, until softened. Stir in the cinnamon, nutmeg, allspice, cloves, cayenne, and ginger, and sauté for 2 minutes longer. Add the stock, season with salt and pepper, and simmer for 20 minutes. Remove from the heat, let cool slightly, and add the half-and-half. Transfer to the food processor and purée with the pumpkin. Return to a clean saucepan and warm through. Adjust the seasonings and ladle into serving bowls. Garnish with the apple.

SERVES: 4

Big, meaty portobellos make a hearty, filling soup. To clean portobellos, wipe with a damp cloth or paper towels; do not wash with water, which would make them soggy. Serve this soup with a good crusty bread.

Grilled Portobello Mushroom–
Sherry Soup

Brush the mushrooms with 2 tablespoons of the oil and grill over direct medium heat until they can be easily pierced with the tip of a sharp knife, about 5 minutes per side. Dice and set aside. Heat the remaining 2 tablespoons of oil in a nonstick skillet pan and sweat the onion and garlic over medium heat for about 7 minutes.

In a heavy saucepan, melt the butter over medium heat and add the flour while stirring, until blended and lightly colored, about 5 minutes. Gradually stir in the beef and vegetable stocks, and add the sherry, bay leaves, parsley, salt, and pepper. Add the cooked mushrooms, onion, and garlic, and warm through. Remove the bay leaves before serving.

SERVES: 4

2 or 3 portobello mushrooms (about 1 pound), cleaned
4 tablespoons olive oil
1 onion, diced
2 cloves garlic, minced
1/4 cup butter
1/2 cup all-purpose flour
2 cups beef stock
2 cups vegetable stock or water
1/4 cup dry sherry
2 bay leaves
1 tablespoon minced flat-leaf parsley
Salt and freshly ground black pepper to taste

There are times when nothing but a large, plainly seasoned steak will do. You can use either mesquite wood chips soaked in water or mesquite charcoal to infuse the robust steaks with flavor. This delicious flavored butter will perk up just about any steak.

Mesquite-Grilled
Porterhouse Steaks
with Oregano-Tomato Butter
& Grilled Garlic Mashed Potatoes

OREGANO-TOMATO STEAK BUTTER

- 3 tablespoons butter, at room temperature
- 1/2 tablespoon tomato paste
- 1 teaspoon freshly squeezed lemon juice (1/2 small lemon)
- 1 tablespoon minced fresh oregano leaves, or 1/2 tablespoon dried
- 1/4 teaspoon freshly ground black pepper

POTATOES

- 1 1/2 pounds Yukon Gold potatoes, peeled and cut in half
- 1 tablespoon puréed grilled garlic (page 113)
- 2 tablespoons butter, at room temperature
- 1/4 cup milk
- 1/4 cup half-and-half (or substitute more milk)
- Salt and freshly ground black pepper to taste

STEAKS

- 4 porterhouse steaks (about 16 ounces each and 1 inch thick), prime or choice grade
- Salt and freshly ground black pepper to taste

Place the 3 tablespoons butter, the tomato paste, lemon juice, oregano, and pepper in a small bowl and mix thoroughly. Transfer to a small ramekin and form into a smooth butter pat. Chill in the refrigerator, and just before serving, divide into 4 pieces.

Place the potatoes in a saucepan of salted water and bring to a boil. Turn down the heat and simmer for about 20 minutes, until tender. Drain, transfer to a mixing bowl, and add the garlic. Meanwhile, in a small saucepan, heat the 2 tablespoons butter, milk, and half-and-half, and bring to a boil. With an electric mixer or wire whisk, whip the potatoes while drizzling in the milk mixture as needed. Season with salt and pepper.

While the potatoes are cooking, bring the steaks to room temperature and season with salt and pepper. Grill over direct medium-high heat for about 5 minutes per side for medium-rare, 6 to 7 minutes for medium, or to the desired doneness. Transfer to serving plates, place the butter in center of each steak and let melt, and serve with the mashed potatoes.
SERVES: 4

The rich flavor of caramelized onions is a natural partner for steaks. The rub used in this recipe makes a great all-purpose seasoning for red meats. If you enjoy blue cheese, sprinkle a little over the steaks, and add sliced tomatoes if you like.

Spice-Rubbed Grilled
Steak Sandwich
with Brandied Caramelized Onions

Place the pepper, coriander, cumin, paprika, garlic salt, chile powder, allspice, cloves, sugar, and oregano in a bowl and combine thoroughly. Lightly score the steak on both sides and place in a baking dish. Coat the steak evenly on both sides with the spice rub. Cover and let sit for at least 2 hours in the refrigerator.

Meanwhile, to prepare the onions, heat the butter in a saucepan and add the onions and garlic. Cook over medium heat for about 15 minutes, or until the onions are browned and caramelized. Add the brandy, carefully ignite, and let flame until the alcohol is burned off. Add the sugar and stock, and cook for 5 minutes longer, or until the onions are just moist. Keep warm.

Shake off any excess rub from the steak and grill over direct medium heat for about 6 minutes per side for medium rare, about 7 minutes for medium, or to the desired doneness. Remove and carve across the grain into thin slices. Toast the rolls lightly on the grill and spread the aïoli on the bottom half of each roll. Place the arugula and then the beef on each roll, top with the caramelized onions, and cut the sandwiches in half on a diagonal.

SERVES: 4

SPICE RUB AND STEAKS

- 1 tablespoon freshly ground black pepper
- 1 tablespoon freshly ground coriander
- 1 tablespoon ground cumin
- 1 tablespoon paprika
- 1/2 tablespoon garlic salt
- 1/2 tablespoon pure red chile powder
- 1/2 tablespoon ground allspice
- 1/2 teaspoon ground cloves
- 1/2 tablespoon brown sugar
- 1 teaspoon dried oregano
- 4 slices beef round sirloin tip (about 8 ounces each), prime or choice grade

ONIONS

- 2 tablespoons butter or olive oil
- 2 large sweet onions (such as Vidalia), sliced
- 1 clove garlic, minced
- 3 tablespoons brandy
- 2 tablespoons brown sugar
- 2 tablespoons beef stock

SANDWICHES

- 4 individual French or whole-wheat rolls, warmed through
- 2 tablespoons Lemon Zest Aïoli (page 108), mayonnaise, or softened butter
- 4 cups arugula

Besides achieving maximum flavor, making sure the garlic and chile slivers are beneath the surface of the steaks also ensures that they won't burn on the grill. If you're not fond of the heat of chiles, by all means use just the garlic slivers.

Garlic and Chile-Stabbed
T-Bone Steaks
with Grilled Corn Relish

RELISH

1 red bell pepper

4 ears fresh sweet corn, husked

3 tablespoons olive oil, divided

$1/4$ cup diced onion

3 tablespoons diced sun-dried tomatoes (packed in oil)

2 scallions, sliced

1 tablespoon freshly squeezed lime juice ($1/2$ large lime)

1 tablespoon sherry vinegar

$1/2$ tablespoon minced marjoram

Salt to taste

STEAKS

4 T-bone steaks (about 1 pound each and 1 inch thick), prime or choice grade

6 cloves garlic, cut lengthwise into thick slivers about $3/8$ inch long

1 serrano chile, seeded and cut lengthwise into thick slivers about $3/8$ inch long

Salt and freshly ground black pepper to taste

To prepare the relish, roast the bell pepper on the grill and let steam (see page 113 to 114). When cool, peel, seed, and dice the pepper, and place in a mixing bowl. While the pepper is cooling, brush the corn with 2 tablespoons of the oil and grill over indirect medium heat for about 15 minutes, turning frequently, until lightly browned on all sides. Remove and, when cool enough to handle, cut the kernels from the cobs and add to the mixing bowl. Heat the remaining 1 tablespoon of oil in a skillet and sauté the onion over medium-high heat for 3 or 4 minutes, until soft. Add the sautéed onions, sun-dried tomatoes, scallions, lime juice, vinegar, and marjoram. Season with salt, and toss to combine.

Using the tip of a sharp paring knife, make incisions in the steaks about $1/2$ inch deep. Insert the garlic and serrano slivers into the incisions, making sure they are embedded beneath the surface of the steaks. Season with salt and pepper and bring the steaks to room temperature. Grill over direct medium-high heat for 5 or 6 minutes per side for medium-rare, 7 to 8 minutes for medium, or to the desired doneness. Serve with the relish.

SERVES: 4

This recipe is for the black pepper lover in all of us. Use the best-quality, freshest peppercorns you can find. You remember those peppercorns you've had lying around on your condiment shelf for a while? Well, don't be tempted to use them here!

Grilled Peppered
Filet Mignon
with Brandy-Peppercorn Sauce

SAUCE

- 3 cups Pinot Noir, Cabernet Sauvignon, or other good-quality, robust red wine
- 3 tablespoons butter, divided
- 2 shallots, minced
- 1/2 tablespoon freshly crushed black peppercorns
- 1/2 cup brandy
- 1/2 cup heavy cream
- 1/2 cup beef stock
- Salt to taste

STEAKS

- 4 filet mignon steaks (about 7 ounces each and 1 1/2 inches thick), prime or choice grade
- 1 tablespoon Dijon mustard
- 3 tablespoons freshly cracked black peppercorns
- 1 tablespoon freshly cracked red peppercorns
- 1/2 tablespoon kosher salt

To prepare the sauce, pour the wine into a nonreactive saucepan and bring to a boil. Let reduce over medium-high heat until about 1/2 cup remains, about 20 minutes. Meanwhile, heat 2 tablespoons of the butter in a small heavy saucepan and sauté the shallots and peppercorns over medium heat for 2 minutes. Add the brandy, carefully ignite, and let flame for 3 or 4 minutes until the alcohol is burned off. Continue cooking for 2 to 3 minutes, until the pan is almost dry. Add the cream, turn up the heat to medium-high, and cook for 3 minutes. Add the stock and cook for 5 minutes. Stir in the reduced wine and cook over medium heat for 10 minutes longer. Stir in the remaining 1 tablespoon of butter, season with salt, and simmer until 1 cup remains, about 10 minutes more.

Meanwhile, bring the steaks to room temperature and brush both sides with the mustard. Combine the peppercorns and salt on a plate and roll the steaks in the mixture, pressing to coat each side well. Grill the steaks over direct medium-high heat for about 5 minutes per side for medium-rare, 6 to 7 minutes for medium, or to the desired doneness. Transfer to serving plates and spoon with the warm sauce over.

SERVES: 4

For best results, use soaked hickory chips to impart a deliciously smoky flavor. And to make sauce, transfer the marinade to a saucepan while grilling the steaks, boil for 5 minutes, strain, swirl in 2 tablespoons of butter, and season with salt and pepper.

Merlot-Marinated
Sirloin Steaks
with Grilled Scallions & Peppers

MARINADE AND STEAKS

- 1/2 cup Merlot
- 2 tablespoons olive oil
- 2 tablespoons Worcestershire sauce
- 2 cloves garlic, minced
- 1 tablespoon chopped fresh thyme leaves
- 2 dried bay leaves, crumbled
- 1 teaspoon freshly ground black pepper
- 4 top sirloin or boneless strip steaks (about 8 ounces each and 1 1/8 inches thick), prime or choice grade

VEGETABLES

- 1/2 cup olive oil
- 2 tablespoons herbes de Provence or mixed dried herbs
- 3 cloves garlic, minced
- 2 red bell peppers, cut lengthwise into quarters and seeded
- 1 yellow bell pepper, cut lengthwise into quarters and seeded
- 1 green bell pepper, cut lengthwise into quarters and seeded
- 8 scallions, trimmed

Place the wine, oil, Worcestershire sauce, garlic, thyme, bay leaves, and pepper in a nonreactive baking dish, stir together, and let sit for 20 minutes for the flavors to blend. Add the steaks, cover with plastic wrap, and let marinate at room temperature for 1 hour, turning the steaks occasionally.

To prepare the vegetables, place the oil, herbs, and garlic in a medium bowl; mix well. Add the bell peppers and scallions. Let marinate for 1 hour, turning occasionally.

Place the bell peppers crosswise over the bars of the grilling grate and arrange the scallions around the peppers, over the edge of the heat source. Grill the vegetables over direct medium-high heat for 8 to 10 minutes, basting lightly with the marinade and turning occasionally; move them away from the heat as necessary. When cooked, remove the vegetables to the edge of the grill, away from direct heat, and keep warm.

Remove the steaks from the marinade and grill over direct medium-high heat for about 4 minutes per side for medium-rare, 5 to 6 minutes for medium, or to the desired doneness. Serve the steaks with the grilled vegetables.
SERVES: 4

Texas and New Mexico are major producers of pecans and chiles, and Chimayo, New Mexico, produces wonderful red chile powder. Instead of broiling the steaks, toast the pecans first in a skillet and finish the crusted steaks on the grill. Serve with a mixed green salad.

Pecan-Crusted
Boneless Strips
with Chimayo Red Chile Sauce

To prepare the sauce, grill the tomatoes over indirect medium-high heat, turning often, until the skins are somewhat cracked and partly blackened, about 15 minutes. (Do not overcook or they will taste bitter.) Remove, coarsely chop (do not peel), and transfer to a blender. Meanwhile, heat the oil in a small skillet and sauté the garlic and onion over medium heat for 5 minutes. Transfer to the blender and add the chile powder, oregano, cumin, and stock. Purée until smooth. Strain into a clean saucepan, bring to a simmer, and cook for 20 minutes, or until thickened. Stir in the butter and keep warm.

Preheat the broiler. To prepare the crust, place the pecans, oil, mustard, honey, and salt in a shallow bowl or dish and whisk gently to mix well. Set aside. Lightly season the steaks with salt (if desired) and pepper and grill over direct medium-high heat for 3 minutes on each side. Transfer to a roasting pan and spread the crust over the top of each steak. Finish under the broiler for 1 or 2 minutes for medium-rare, 4 minutes for medium, or to the desired doneness. Ladle the sauce onto serving plates, top with the steaks, crust-side up, and garnish each steak with a chile.

SERVES: 4

SAUCE

- 12 ounces plum tomatoes
- 1 tablespoon olive oil
- 2 cloves garlic, minced
- 1/4 cup minced onion
- 2 tablespoons mild or medium pure red chile powder (preferably Chimayo)
- 1 teaspoon dried oregano
- 1 teaspoon toasted ground cumin (page 32)
- 1 1/2 cups vegetable stock
- 1 tablespoon butter (optional)

CRUST AND STEAKS

- 1 cup pecan pieces, finely minced
- 2 tablespoons olive oil
- 2 tablespoons Dijon mustard
- 1 tablespoon honey
- 1/4 teaspoon salt
- 4 boneless strip steaks (about 8 ounces each and 7/8-inch thick), prime or choice grade
- Salt and freshly ground black pepper to taste
- 4 red serrano or small red jalapeño chiles for garnish

Chipotle chiles—dried, smoked jalapeños—can be purchased dried or canned in a spicy adobo sauce. Since dried chiles need to be rehydrated for 20 minutes in warm water, we prefer the convenience of canned—and the adobo sauce is extremely flavorful.

Chipotle Grilled Filets
with Black Bean-Roasted Mango Salsa

Place the oil, chiles, lime juice, honey, garlic, cilantro, and salt in a blender and purée until smooth. Transfer to a nonreactive baking dish and add the steaks. Let marinate at room temperature for 30 minutes.

Meanwhile, to prepare the salsa, grill the mango slices over direct medium heat for 5 minutes. (Use a grilling basket or set the slices on a metal rack placed at 90 degrees to the grilling rack.) Remove, dice, and transfer to a mixing bowl. Add the beans, bell pepper, scallions, chile, cilantro, and lime juice. Season with salt.

Remove the steaks from the marinade and grill over direct medium-high heat for 4 to 5 minutes for medium-rare, about 6 minutes for medium, or to the desired doneness. Serve with the salsa.

SERVES: 4

MARINADE AND STEAKS

- 1/4 cup olive oil
- 3 tablespoons canned chipotle chiles in adobo sauce
- 3 tablespoons freshly squeezed lime juice (2 medium limes)
- 1 tablespoon honey
- 1 tablespoon grilled garlic (page 113)
- 1/4 cup chopped fresh cilantro leaves
- Pinch of salt
- 4 filet mignon steaks (about 6 ounces each and 1 1/4 inches thick), prime or choice grade

SALSA

- 2 mangoes, peeled and cut lengthwise around the pit into slices
- 1 1/2 cups cooked and drained black beans (or canned and drained)
- 1/4 cup diced red bell pepper
- 2 scallions, green and white parts, sliced
- 1/2 jalapeño chile, seeded and minced
- 1/2 tablespoon minced fresh cilantro leaves
- 1 tablespoon freshly squeezed lime juice (1/2 large lime)
- Salt to taste

Use your favorite barbecue sauce for the burgers or make the recipe on page 52. You may want to make the burgers first and let them sit before grilling them while you prepare the onions. That way, the onions need to be kept warm for less time after cooking.

Jarlsberg Cheese, Bacon &
Chile Burgers
with Crispy Sweet Onions

ONIONS

2 to 3 cups vegetable oil

1 cup all-purpose flour

1/2 cup cornstarch

1/2 teaspoon salt plus additional to taste

1/2 teaspoon freshly ground black pepper

4 large sweet onions, finely julienned

BURGERS

1 1/2 pounds lean, high-quality ground beef

2 cloves garlic, minced

1/2 cup minced red onion

1/4 cup minced fresh parsley leaves

1 1/2 tablespoons hot chile sauce (such as Melinda's or Tabasco)

1 tablespoon barbecue or Worcestershire sauce

1 egg, beaten

Salt and freshly ground black pepper to taste

4 slices Jarlsberg or Swiss cheese (about 1 1/2 ounces each)

8 slices bacon, cut in half

4 whole wheat hamburger buns

4 romaine lettuce leaves

To prepare the onions, heat the oil in a deep-fryer or heavy saucepan. (It should come at least 2 inches up the sides.) Place the flour, cornstarch, salt, and pepper on a plate, mix, and lightly dredge the onions in the mixture. When the oil is hot (about 350°F), fry the onions 5 minutes over medium-high heat, turning gently and often, until golden brown. Drain on paper towels, keep warm, and season with additional salt.

To prepare the burgers, place the beef, garlic, onion, parsley, chile sauce, barbecue sauce, egg, salt, and pepper in a mixing bowl. With your hands, mix well and form into 4 patties about 3/4 inch thick. Grill over direct medium-high heat for 6 minutes per side, or until cooked through to medium and the internal temperature reaches 160°F (see page 115). About 2 minutes before removing from the grill, place cheese on top of each burger and melt.

Meanwhile, sauté the bacon in a dry skillet over medium heat until cooked through but not crispy, about 2 to 3 minutes per side. Remove and drain on paper towels. Split each bun in half and grill or toast. Place the romaine on the bottom half of each bun and top with the burgers. Place the bacon on top of each burger in a criss-cross pattern and top with the other half of the bun. Serve with the onions. SERVES: 4

Teriyaki is the Japanese term for preparing meat in a soy-based marinade before cooking, often on the grill. Brushing the beef with the cooked marinade while it is grilling enhances the flavor of the dish and keeps the meat moist, but is optional.

Teriyaki Tenderloin
Beef Kabobs
with Sticky White Rice

To prepare the marinade, place all ingredients except the beef in a saucepan and heat through, whisking until the sugar dissolves. Let cool. Transfer to a mixing bowl, add the beef, and marinate in the refrigerator 2 to 3 hours, turning occasionally.

Place the rice in a strainer and pour running cold water over it until the water no longer looks milky. Soak in a bowl of water for 1 hour. Drain and transfer to a saucepan, together with the 2 cups of cold water. Bring to a boil, turn the heat to low, and cover. Simmer about 15 minutes, or until the water has been absorbed and the rice is sticky and soft. Keep warm.

Drain the beef and thread onto metal or bamboo skewers that have been soaked in water for 30 minutes. (Using two parallel skewers instead of one prevents the meat from spinning around and not cooking evenly.) Pour the marinade into a saucepan and bring to a boil. Cook over medium-high heat 5 minutes, until reduced and syrupy. Grill the kabobs over direct medium-high heat for 8 to 10 minutes, turning occasionally, brushing the meat with the marinade glaze with each turn.

Remove the beef from the skewers and transfer to serving plates with the rice.

SERVES: 4

MARINADE AND BEEF

- 3/4 cup soy sauce
- 1/2 cup sherry
- 3 tablespoons sake (optional)
- 3 tablespoons unseasoned rice wine vinegar
- 3 tablespoons brown sugar
- 3 cloves garlic, minced
- 1 tablespoon peeled and minced fresh ginger
- 1 scallion, sliced
- 1 teaspoon crushed red pepper flakes, or to taste
- 1 1/2 pounds tenderloin tips or boneless strip steaks, choice grade, cut into 1-inch cubes

RICE

- 2 cups short-grain white rice
- 2 cups cold water

Once you taste this rub, you'll return to this recipe again and again! Polenta is a staple of northern Italy, and the best we've tried was in Cremona, between Milan and Parma. If you prefer, use 6 cups stock in the polenta, and omit the milk.

Sweet-Rub
Rib-Eye Steaks
with Grilled Polenta Cremona-Style

POLENTA

4 cups chicken stock
  or water

2 cups milk

1¼ cups cornmeal

1 teaspoon paprika

1 teaspoon salt

1 teaspoon freshly
  cracked black pepper

2 tablespoons plus
  1 teaspoon butter

RUB AND STEAKS

2 tablespoons
  brown sugar

1½ tablespoons freshly
  cracked black pepper

1½ tablespoons paprika

1 tablespoon
  ground cumin

½ tablespoon salt

4 rib-eye steaks
  (8 ounces each and
  about 1 inch thick),
  prime or choice grade

To prepare the polenta, bring the stock and milk to a boil in a large saucepan over high heat. Add the cornmeal in a steady, gradual stream, whisking continuously to prevent lumps. Boil for 1 or 2 minutes. Turn down the heat to low and whisk almost continuously for about 30 minutes, or until the mixture begins to thicken considerably. Stir in the paprika, salt, pepper, and 2 tablespoons of the butter, and transfer to a greased 9-inch square baking pan, spreading with a spatula to make an even layer. Let chill in the refrigerator for 4 hours or overnight, until firm.

To prepare the rub, combine the sugar, pepper, paprika, cumin, and salt on a platter and coat the steaks with the mixture. Let sit in the refrigerator for 30 minutes, then bring to room temperature.

Turn out the chilled polenta and cut into squares or right-angled triangles. In a small saucepan, melt the remaining teaspoon of butter (or substitute 1 teaspoon olive oil), brush on the polenta, and grill over direct medium-high heat for about 4 or 5 minutes on each side, or until lightly browned.

Grill the steaks over direct medium-high heat for 4 to 5 minutes for medium-rare, about 6 minutes for medium, or to the desired doneness. Serve with the polenta.

SERVES: 4

You can leave the barbecue sauce unstrained if you wish. If you do strain it, the remaining onion mixture makes a tasty side for this or another barbecued dish. Other good sides with this recipe are beans (see page 60) and cornbread (see page 72).

Chile-Rubbed BBQ Hickory Pork Ribs
with Down-Home BBQ Sauce

RUB AND RIBS

- ¹/₂ cup pure red chile powder
- 2 tablespoons dried red pepper flakes
- 2 teaspoons brown sugar
- 2 teaspoons dried oregano
- 2 teaspoons garlic salt
- 3 pounds baby back ribs, trimmed of fat and membrane
- 1 tablespoon olive oil

BBQ SAUCE

- 1 tablespoon olive oil
- 2 onions, diced
- 2 cloves garlic, minced
- 2 jalapeño chiles, seeded and minced
- 2 cups tomato ketchup
- ³/₄ cup dark brown sugar
- ¹/₂ cup red wine vinegar
- 2 tablespoons Worcestershire sauce
- 2 tablespoons steak sauce (such as A-1)
- 1 tablespoon chipotle chile purée (page 114) or mustard
- 1 teaspoon freshly squeezed lemon juice (¹/₂ small lemon)

Place the chile powder, pepper flakes, sugar, oregano, and salt in a mixing bowl and stir until the sugar dissolves. Brush the ribs with the olive oil and then coat with the rub on both sides. Transfer to a platter and let sit in the refrigerator to marinate for 3 or 4 hours, or overnight. Bring the ribs to room temperature before grilling.

Add some soaked hickory chips or chunks to a medium grill. Place the ribs, meat-side up, over indirect heat. Cover the grill, vent it slightly, and cook for about 1¹/₄ hours, turning occasionally.

Meanwhile, prepare the sauce. Heat the olive oil in a saucepan and sauté the onions, garlic, and jalapeños over medium-high heat for 4 to 5 minutes, until softened. Add the ketchup, sugar, vinegar, Worcestershire and steak sauces, and chile purée, and bring to a boil. Turn down the heat and gently simmer for 25 minutes, stirring occasionally. Strain the sauce into a clean saucepan if you wish, pressing down with a wooden spoon to make sure all the sauce is separated from the solids. Add the lemon juice and keep warm.

Brush the sauce on the ribs frequently during the last 30 minutes of cooking. The ribs are done when no pink shows when the ribs are pierced with a sharp knife. Slice and serve with the sauce.

SERVES: 4

Orzo is a rice-shaped pasta that looks like grains of barley, which is what the Italian word orzo means. The mushrooms make an elegant partner for both the orzo and pork. Brining, like marinating, is a traditional moisture-preserving method of preparing pork.

Spice & Herb-Brined
Pork Filets
with Wild Mushroom Orzo

To prepare the marinade, place the water, sugar, vinegar, onion, garlic, peppercorns, salt, pepper flakes, thyme, oregano, cumin, and bay leaves in a large nonreactive baking dish and combine. Add the pork and marinate for at least 4 hours and preferably overnight.

To prepare the orzo, place the stock and water in a saucepan and bring to a boil. Add the orzo and return to a boil. Turn down the heat and simmer for 8 to 10 minutes, until al dente. Meanwhile, heat the oil in a medium skillet and sauté the shallots for 2 minutes. Add the mushrooms and sauté for 5 or 6 minutes, or until the mushrooms are tender and have released their liquid. Season with salt and pepper. Drain the orzo and stir in the wild mushroom mixture.

Meanwhile, remove the pork from the marinade and grill over direct medium-high heat for 4 to 5 minutes on each side for medium-well, or until the internal temperature reaches 160°F to 170°F (see page 115). Transfer to warm serving plates and serve with the orzo. Garnish the orzo with the parsley.

SERVES: 4

MARINADE AND PORK

- 2 cups warm water
- 1/2 cup sugar
- 1/4 cup white wine vinegar
- 1 onion, chopped
- 3 cloves garlic, sliced
- 1 tablespoon crushed black peppercorns
- 1 tablespoon salt
- 1 tablespoon dried red pepper flakes (optional)
- 1 tablespoon dried thyme
- 1/2 tablespoon dried oregano
- 1/2 tablespoon ground cumin
- 2 bay leaves, crumbled
- 1 1/2 pounds pork tenderloin, cut crosswise into 8 filets of 3 ounces each

ORZO

- 3 cups chicken stock
- 2 cups water
- 2 cups dried orzo pasta
- 2 tablespoons olive oil
- 2 tablespoons finely minced shallots
- 6 ounces wild mushrooms (preferably morels, chanterelles, or shiitakes), diced
- Salt and freshly ground black pepper to taste
- 2 tablespoons minced flat-leaf parsley for garnish

This is perfect for a light summer lunch or dinner, and shows just how well pork and fruit go together. Out of season, use freshly dried (and preferably unsulfured) apricots. Use ready-cut, 4-ounce pork medallions instead of whole loin if you prefer.

Grilled Marinated
Pork Medallions
with Apricots & Golden Raisins

To prepare the marinade, whisk together the oil, sugar, herbs, salt, and pepper in a mixing bowl and transfer to a nonreactive loaf pan or baking dish. Add the pork tenderloins and marinate in the refrigerator for 2 hours, turning occasionally. Remove and bring to room temperature.

To prepare the fruit, place the apricots, raisins, wine, honey, and lemon zest in a saucepan and bring to a boil over medium-high heat. Reduce the heat to medium-low and simmer, uncovered, for 15 minutes. Stir in the cream and warm through for 5 minutes; do not boil.

Remove the pork tenderloins from the marinade, draining any excess liquid. Grill over direct medium-high heat for 10 to 12 minutes on each side, or until the internal temperature reaches 160°F to 170°F (see page 115). Cut each piece of loin into 3 medallions and transfer to serving plates. Spoon the fruit and sauce over and around the medallions.

SERVES: 4

MARINADE AND PORK

- 1 cup extra virgin olive oil
- 1 tablespoon brown sugar
- 1 tablespoon herbes de Provence or dried mixed herbs
- 1/2 teaspoon salt
- 1/2 teaspoon freshly ground black pepper
- 2 pork tenderloins (about 12 ounces each), cut in half crosswise

APRICOTS AND RAISINS

- 8 apricots, cut in half and pitted, or 12 dried apricots
- 1/4 cup golden raisins
- 1 1/2 cups white wine
- 2 teaspoons honey
- 1/2 tablespoon minced lemon zest
- 1/3 cup heavy cream

This is a wonderful dish for chile lovers, although you can omit the Tabasco and still serve a delicious meal. Alternatively, if you really enjoy heat, use a habanero chile sauce, but be forewarned: a little of the ultra-hot habanero goes a long way!

Citrus-Marinated
Pork Loin
with Mango-Chile Sauce

MARINADE AND PORK

1 cup olive oil

2 shallots, minced

1 tablespoon minced garlic

Juice of 2 oranges

Juice of 2 limes

1 tablespoon chopped fresh cilantro leaves

1/2 teaspoon salt

1 tablespoon crushed black peppercorns

1 1/2 pounds pork loin

SAUCE

2 cups mango nectar or thawed and puréed frozen mango

1/4 cup unseasoned rice wine vinegar

1/4 cup chicken stock or water

2 teaspoons Tabasco sauce or Tabasco-Garlic sauce, or to taste

1 teaspoon sugar

1/4 teaspoon salt

To prepare the marinade, heat the oil, shallots, and garlic in a saucepan. Sauté over medium heat for 4 to 5 minutes and then pour into a nonreactive loaf pan or baking dish. Let cool slightly and add the citrus juices, cilantro, salt, and peppercorns. Stir to combine and add the pork loin. Marinate in the refrigerator for 2 hours, turning occasionally if not covered by the marinade. Remove and bring to room temperature.

To prepare the sauce, place the mango nectar, vinegar, stock, Tabasco, sugar, and salt in a saucepan and bring to a boil. Turn down the heat and simmer over medium-low heat for 15 minutes, uncovered, or until the sauce has reduced a little and thickened. Keep warm.

Heat a dry heavy skillet over medium-high heat for 5 minutes. Drain any excess liquid from the pork loin and sear on all sides, about 3 to 4 minutes. Transfer to the grill and cook, covered, over indirect medium heat for about 10 minutes on each side, or until the internal temperature reaches 160°F to 170°F (see page 115). Cut the loin into 6 or 8 slices and transfer to serving plates. Spoon the sauce over and around the pork.

SERVES: 4

Hoisin sauce, a Chinese condiment made from fermented soybean paste, chiles, spices, and garlic, is both sweet and spicy—and is almost addictive! It makes a wonderful base for a rib glaze and blends perfectly with the other Asian flavors.

Hong Kong
Pork Ribs
with Spicy Hoisin-Ginger Glaze

To prepare the marinade, place the soy sauce, sugar, sake, scallions, cilantro, garlic, and ginger in a large nonreactive baking dish and stir until the sugar dissolves. Add the ribs and marinate in the refrigerator for at least 4 hours, and preferably overnight. Bring the ribs to room temperature before grilling.

To prepare the glaze, place the hoisin sauce, ketchup, honey, soy sauce, sake, vinegar, chile sauce, and ginger in a saucepan and bring to a simmer. Cook for about 15 minutes, uncovered, until thickened. Keep warm.

Drain any excess marinade from the ribs and place on the grill meat side up. Cover the grill, vent it slightly, and cook over indirect heat for about 1 to 1¼ hours, turning occasionally. Brush the glaze on the ribs frequently during the last 30 minutes of cooking time. Slice the ribs just before serving and serve with the remaining warm glaze.

SERVES: 4

MARINADE AND RIBS

1 cup soy sauce

½ cup brown sugar

¼ cup sake or dry sherry

2 tablespoons
  sliced scallions

2 tablespoons minced
  fresh cilantro leaves

1 tablespoon
  minced garlic

1 tablespoon peeled and
  minced fresh ginger

4 pounds pork spare ribs,
  trimmed of fat and
  membrane

GLAZE

½ cup hoisin sauce

½ cup tomato ketchup

¼ cup honey

¼ cup soy sauce

¼ cup sake or dry sherry

2 tablespoons
  unseasoned
  rice wine vinegar

2 tablespoons Asian
  chile sauce with garlic
  (such as sambal oelek)

1 tablespoon peeled and
  minced fresh ginger

Grilling particularly enhances the fruity and smoky flavors of this spicy glaze. Note that the baked-beans recipe includes the shortcut of canned beans as a base for the complex flavors that are added. By all means use home-cooked beans instead.

Sweet-Rubbed Raspberry-Glazed Ribs
with BBQ Beans

GLAZE AND RIBS

- 1 1/2 cups seedless raspberry jam
- 1/4 cup puréed canned chipotle chiles in adobo sauce (page 114)
- 1/4 cup apple cider vinegar
- 2 teaspoons puréed grilled garlic (page 113), or 2 cloves garlic, minced
- 1/2 tablespoon salt
- 3 pounds baby back ribs, trimmed of fat and membrane

BEANS

- 3 slices bacon, chopped
- 1 onion, diced
- 1 jalapeño chile, seeded and minced
- 2 cloves garlic, minced
- 1/4 cup tomato ketchup
- 1/4 cup dark molasses
- 2 tablespoons Dijon mustard
- 1 tablespoon Worcestershire sauce
- 1/2 tablespoon apple cider vinegar
- Salt and freshly ground black pepper to taste
- 2 cans (14 ounces each) white beans or pinto beans, drained

To prepare the glaze, place the jam, chipotle chiles, vinegar, garlic, and salt in a mixing bowl and thoroughly combine. Place the ribs in a nonreactive baking dish and pour the glaze over. Let marinate in the refrigerator for 3 or 4 hours.

Remove the ribs from the glaze and let excess liquid drain off the ribs; transfer the glaze to a saucepan. Place the ribs, meat-side up, over indirect medium heat. Cover the grill, vent it slightly, and cook for about 1 1/4 hours, turning occasionally. Brush the glaze on the ribs frequently during the last 30 minutes of cooking time. The ribs are done when no pink meat shows when the ribs are pierced with a sharp knife. Boil the glaze gently for 5 minutes; keep warm.

Sauté the bacon over medium heat in a large dry saucepan until cooked through but not crispy, about 2 to 3 minutes per side. Remove with a slotted spoon and drain on paper towels. Place the onion, jalapeño, and garlic in the pan and sauté over medium-high heat for 3 minutes. Add the cooked bacon, ketchup, molasses, mustard, Worcestershire sauce, vinegar, salt, and pepper and bring to a boil. Add the beans and simmer for 15 minutes, until heated through.

Slice the cooked ribs and serve with the beans and the cooked glaze on the side.

SERVES: 4

Free-form patties are much more convenient than using sausage casings. You can substitute 1/2 teaspoon dried red pepper flakes for the fresh chiles. Grill the tomatoes and sausages simultaneously, with the sausages over direct heat and the tomatoes to the side.

Grandma's Grilled Pork
Sausage Patties
with Grilled Tomatoes

To prepare the sausages, place the pork, beef, bacon, garlic, chiles, breadcrumbs, sage, salt, cumin, pepper, and egg in a mixing bowl and thoroughly combine. Divide the mixture into 12 portions and form into small patties. Transfer to a platter, cover, and let sit in the refrigerator for 1 hour.

Meanwhile, cut the tops off the tomatoes and remove some of the pulp and seeds to form a cavity in the middles. Pour in the olive oil and sprinkle with the basil and garlic. Let sit for 30 minutes.

Grill the tomatoes over indirect medium heat for 12 to 15 minutes, or until grilled through. Grill the sausages over direct medium-high heat for 7 to 8 minutes per side, or until cooked through and the internal temperature reaches 160°F to 170° (see page 115). Serve the sausages with the tomatoes and garnish the sausages with the sage sprigs.

SERVES: 4

SAUSAGES

- 1 pound lean high-quality ground pork
- 8 ounces lean high-quality ground beef
- 3 slices bacon, finely diced (optional)
- 2 cloves garlic, minced
- 2 red serrano chiles or 1 red jalapeño, seeded and minced (optional)
- 1/4 cup fresh breadcrumbs
- 1 tablespoon minced fresh sage leaves
- 1/2 teaspoon salt
- 1/2 teaspoon ground cumin
- 1/4 teaspoon freshly ground black pepper
- 1 egg, beaten

TOMATOES

- 8 vine-ripened tomatoes
- 1/4 cup olive oil
- 4 teaspoons minced fresh basil leaves
- 1 teaspoon minced garlic
- 4 sprigs fresh sage for garnish

Praise be for Louisiana, whose rich and mixed culture gave the world both Creole and Cajun cuisines! You won't need all of the multipurpose Creole seasoning for this recipe, but save the extra in an airtight container for other uses.

Creole-Style Seasoned Pork
with Honey-Mustard Grilled Peaches

CREOLE SEASONING AND PORK

- 1 tablespoon paprika
- 2 teaspoons celery salt or kosher salt
- 2 teaspoons garlic powder
- 2 teaspoons pure red chile powder, or to taste
- 1/2 tablespoon onion powder
- 1/2 tablespoon dried marjoram or oregano
- 1/2 tablespoon dried thyme
- 1 teaspoon freshly ground black pepper
- 1 teaspoon freshly ground white pepper
- 4 pork rib chops (about 12 ounces each and 1 to 1 1/4 inches thick)

PEACHES

- 2 tablespoons freshly squeezed lime juice (1 large lime)
- 1 tablespoon honey
- 1/2 tablespoon sugar
- 2 teaspoons Dijon mustard
- 6 peaches (preferably freestone), cut in half and pitted

Place the paprika, celery salt, garlic powder, chile powder, onion powder, marjoram, thyme, and black and white peppers in a mixing bowl. Season each chop with about 3/4 teaspoon of the seasoning mixture. Let the chops sit for a few minutes.

Grill the chops over direct medium-high heat for about 6 minutes per side for medium, 7 to 8 minutes for medium-well, or until the internal temperature reaches 160°F to 170°F (see page 115).

While the chops are grilling, mix together the lime juice, honey, sugar, and mustard in a bowl. Brush the peaches with the mixture and place, cut-side down, on the grill over indirect medium heat. After 3 or 4 minutes, turn the peaches over and brush with the lime juice mixture. Grill for about 2 or 3 minutes longer, or until cooked through. Serve with the grilled chops.

SERVES: 4

Feel free to substitute any available fresh herbs, such as thyme, basil, or marjoram. For a shortcut with the relish—a zippy alternative to the traditional apple sauce—use frozen chopped green chiles, thawed. Serve with a slotted spoon, or drain first.

Fresh Herb-Crusted
Pork Chops
with Roasted Green Chile-Apple Relish

RELISH

4 fresh green
   New Mexico or
   Anaheim chiles

1/2 cup apple cider

2 apples (preferably
   Granny Smith), peeled,
   cored, and diced

1/2 red bell pepper,
   seeded and diced

1/2 tablespoon minced
   fresh oregano leaves

1 teaspoon sugar

1/2 tablespoon peanut oil

2 teaspoons freshly
   squeezed lime juice
   (1/2 medium lime)

Pinch of salt

HERB CRUST AND PORK

4 tablespoons chopped
   fresh sage leaves

4 tablespoons chopped
   fresh oregano leaves

4 tablespoons chopped
   fresh tarragon leaves

4 tablespoons chopped
   fresh flat-leaf parsley

1/4 cup olive oil

1/2 teaspoon
   minced garlic

1/2 teaspoon salt

1/2 teaspoon freshly
   ground black pepper

4 center-cut pork loin
   chops (about 8 ounces
   each and 1 inch thick)

To prepare the relish, roast the chiles on the grill and let steam (see page 113 to 114). When cool, peel, seed, and dice, and transfer to a mixing bowl. While the chiles are steaming, heat the apple cider in a saucepan and bring to a boil. Add the apples and poach over medium-low heat for 5 minutes, or until soft but not mushy. Transfer to the mixing bowl. Add the bell pepper, oregano, sugar, oil, lime juice, and salt, and gently combine. Set aside. (Keep refrigerated if not using immediately.)

To prepare the crust, place the herbs, oil, garlic, salt, and pepper in a food processor or blender and purée. Transfer to a mixing bowl.

Grill the chops over direct medium-high heat for 3 minutes on each side. Remove from the grill and let cool slightly. Score the chops on each side, rub in the herb crust, and cover the meat with it. Return to the grill and cook for about 4 minutes longer on each side for medium-well, or until the internal temperature reaches 160°F to 170°F (see page 115). Transfer to warm plates and serve with the relish.

SERVES: 4

Lamb and mint are natural partners (but we prefer the more subtle flavors of this marinade to the often-overused mint jelly), and as the Greek dish moussaka proves, so are lamb and eggplant. We bring all three ingredients together in this tasty dish.

Citrus-Mint Marinated Boneless
Leg of Lamb
with Grilled Eggplant Salad

For the marinade, place the oil and lime juice in a mixing bowl and whisk together. Add the mint, garlic, vinegar, salt, and pepper. Place the lamb in a nonreactive baking dish or shallow bowl and pour the marinade over. Let sit in the refrigerator overnight (or at least 6 hours), turning occasionally.

To prepare the salad, whisk together the oil, vinegar, lime juice, and garlic in a bowl. Brush the peppers and eggplant with the dressing and grill over direct medium-high heat, turning and brushing with the dressing until the eggplant slices are browned and the peppers are seared, about 15 minutes. Reserve the remaining dressing. Set the eggplant and peppers aside, and peel the peppers when they are cool enough to handle.

Remove the lamb from the marinade and drain any excess liquid. Transfer to the grill over a drip pan. Cover the grill, vent it slightly, and cook over indirect medium heat for 50 to 60 minutes for medium-rare (or until the internal temperature reaches 140°F; see page 115), 60 to 75 minutes for medium (150°F; see page 115), or to the desired doneness, turning occasionally. Remove the lamb from the grill and let rest for 10 minutes.

While the lamb is grilling, arrange the eggplant in one layer on the side of each plate. Top with the pepper quarters and the greens. Drizzle with the remaining dressing and garnish with the mint sprigs. Slice the lamb and serve.

SERVES: 4

MARINADE AND LAMB

- 1 cup olive oil
- 1/2 cup freshly squeezed lime juice (4 large limes)
- 1/2 cup minced chopped fresh mint or rosemary leaves
- 2 tablespoons minced garlic
- 2 tablespoons balsamic vinegar
- 2 teaspoons salt
- 1 teaspoon freshly ground black pepper
- 1 boneless leg of lamb (about 4 pounds), choice grade, butterflied

SALAD

- 6 tablespoons extra virgin olive oil
- 3 tablespoons white wine vinegar
- 1 tablespoon freshly squeezed lime juice (1/2 large lime)
- 1/2 teaspoon minced garlic
- 2 red bell peppers, peeled, seeded, and cut into quarters
- 1 eggplant, about 12 ounces, trimmed and sliced about 1/2 inch thick
- 8 cups mesclun greens
- 4 sprigs fresh mint for garnish

This dish successfully combines elements from opposite sides of the Mediterranean. Souvlaki is the Greek dish of skewered, grilled marinated lamb, while couscous is a North African classic that's traditionally served with grilled or roasted lamb.

Aegean Island
Souvlaki
with Grilled Vegetable Couscous

SOUVLAKI

1/2 cup extra virgin olive oil

2 tablespoons minced fresh oregano leaves

1 clove garlic, minced

Salt and freshly ground black pepper to taste

1 1/2 pounds boneless shoulder of lamb, or lamb loin, diced into 1-inch pieces

COUSCOUS

1 red bell pepper

1 small eggplant (about 8 ounces), sliced in half lengthwise

2 small zucchini (about 8 ounces), sliced in half lengthwise

1 small red onion, sliced

Salt to taste

3 1/2 tablespoons olive oil, divided

1 1/2 cups water

1 cup couscous

1/2 cup black olives (such as kalamata), pitted and chopped

4 tablespoons minced fresh flat-leaf parsley, divided

1/4 cup freshly squeezed lemon juice (1 to 2 medium lemons)

1/2 teaspoon minced lemon zest

Place the oil, oregano, garlic, salt, and pepper in a nonreactive baking dish. Add the lamb and marinate, refrigerated, overnight.

To prepare the couscous, roast the bell pepper on the grill and let steam (see page 113 to 114). When cool, peel, seed, dice, and set aside. Meanwhile, lay the eggplant, zucchini, and onion on a work surface, sprinkle with salt, and brush both sides with 3 tablespoons of the oil. Grill the vegetables over direct medium-high heat for 3 or 4 minutes per side. When cool, chop the vegetables and set aside with the peppers. Place the water and a pinch of salt in a saucepan and bring to a boil. Add the remaining 1/2 tablespoon of oil and the couscous; stir once, and remove from the heat. Cover the pan and let sit for 10 minutes to allow the couscous to absorb the liquid.

Remove the lamb from the marinade and thread onto 2 parallel skewers. (If using bamboo skewers, soak in water for 30 minutes to prevent burning.) Grill over direct medium-high heat for 7 or 8 minutes, turning occasionally. Transfer to serving plates. Add the diced vegetables, olives, 3 tablespoons of the parsley, lemon juice, and lemon zest to the couscous, and fluff with a fork. Serve with the lamb skewers, and garnish with the remaining tablespoon of parsley.

SERVES: 4

If you prefer, grill the whole rack, then cut into double chops (allow 5 or 6 minutes per side for medium-rare). Harissa is a North African condiment made with chiles and traditionally served with lamb and couscous, such as Grilled Vegetable Couscous (see page 66).

Rosemary-Rubbed
Lamb Chops
with Tunisian-Style Harissa

HARISSA

- 2 red bell peppers
- 2 red New Mexico chiles, or 5 red jalapeño chiles
- 1 teaspoon Tabasco sauce
- 2 cloves garlic, chopped
- 3 tablespoons olive oil
- 1/2 tablespoon ground coriander
- 1/2 tablespoon ground cumin
- 1/2 tablespoon ground caraway

LAMB AND RUB

- 1 rack of lamb (8 ribs, about 2 pounds total), trimmed of fat
- 1/3 cup minced fresh rosemary
- 2 tablespoons minced garlic
- 1 tablespoon extra virgin olive oil
- 1 tablespoon freshly squeezed lemon juice (1/2 small lemon)
- 1/2 teaspoon salt
- 1/4 teaspoon freshly ground black pepper
- 6 sprigs rosemary

To prepare the harissa, grill the bell peppers and chiles over direct medium-high heat, remove, and let steam (see page 113 to 114). When cool, peel, seed, and chop the peppers and chiles and transfer to a blender. Add the Tabasco, garlic, oil, coriander, cumin, and caraway, and purée to a paste. Cover and set aside.

Cut the lamb into 4 double chops. To prepare the rub, combine the minced rosemary, garlic, oil, lemon juice, salt, and pepper in a bowl and rub the lamb all over with the mixture. Let sit for 15 minutes at room temperature.

Add 2 or 3 of the rosemary sprigs to the fire before grilling the lamb, and add the remaining sprigs in 1 or 2 turns as the lamb grills. Grill the lamb over direct medium-high heat for 5 to 6 minutes per side for medium-rare, 6 to 7 minutes for medium, or to the desired doneness. Serve the chops with the harissa.

SERVES: 4

The marinade gives the lamb a zing, and the chutney recipe, courtesy of acclaimed chef Mark Miller, owner of Coyote Cafe in Santa Fe, provides a cooling, fruity contrast. Use 4 double rib chops instead of the steaks if you prefer.

Red Wine-Citrus Marinated
Lamb Chops
with Mark's Mango Chutney

For the marinade, place the wine and sugar in a saucepan and bring just to a boil. Remove from the heat and let cool for 15 minutes. Stir in the garlic, orange juice, lemon juice, pepper, and salt, and transfer to a nonreactive loaf pan or baking dish. Add the lamb and let marinate in the refrigerator for 2 hours, turning often. Bring to room temperature.

Meanwhile, to prepare the chutney, heat the oil in a saucepan and sauté the shallots and ginger over medium heat for 5 minutes. Add the mangoes, sugar, and pepper flakes and sauté until tender but not mushy, about 5 minutes longer. Deglaze the pan with the vinegar and reduce the liquid until the ingredients have thickened, about 7 or 8 minutes. Fold in the mint and salt and let cool to room temperature.

Grill the lamb over direct medium-high heat for 4 minutes per side for medium-rare, about 5 minutes for medium, or to the desired doneness. Serve with the chutney.

SERVES: 4

MARINADE AND LAMB

- 1 cup red wine (preferably Pinot Noir)
- 3 tablespoons dark brown sugar
- 1 tablespoon minced garlic
- 1/4 cup freshly squeezed orange juice (1 small orange)
- 1/4 cup freshly squeezed lemon juice (1 to 2 medium lemons)
- 1/2 teaspoon freshly ground black pepper
- 1/2 teaspoon salt
- 4 lamb shoulder steaks (about 8 ounces each and 1 inch thick)

CHUTNEY

- 1 tablespoon peanut oil
- 2 shallots, minced
- 1 tablespoon peeled and grated fresh ginger
- 2 mangoes, peeled, pitted, and diced (about 2 cups)
- 1/4 cup sugar
- 1 tablespoon dried red pepper flakes
- 1/4 cup champagne vinegar
- 6 tablespoons minced fresh mint leaves
- 1/2 teaspoon salt

Halving the racks results in more of the flavors reaching the meat and shortens the grilling time a little. The marinade is not only for flavor, but also to adhere the crust. For smaller appetites or for a lighter meal, cut the lamb and crust ingredients by half.

Pine Nut-Crusted
Rack of Lamb
with Grilled Asparagus

To prepare the marinade, place the mustard, honey, molasses, vermouth, and garlic in a large nonreactive baking dish and mix thoroughly. Score the lamb with a knife between each chop; cover with the marinade and rub in. Let sit in the refrigerator 4 hours, turning occasionally.

Preheat the oven to 325°F. Remove the lamb from the marinade and reserve; bring to room temperature. Grill, fat-side down first, over direct medium-high heat for 5 minutes on each side, or until well seared. Using tongs, hold the racks vertically over the flame to sear ends. Remove from the grill and let cool for 7 or 8 minutes.

Meanwhile, to prepare the crust, place the nuts and breadcrumbs in a food processor and grind finely. Transfer to a shallow bowl and add the oil, salt, and pepper. When the lamb is cool enough to handle, dip in the reserved marinade and then into the crust, pressing to the meat. Transfer to a roasting pan and finish in the oven for 12 to 14 minutes for medium-rare (or an internal temperature of 150°F; see page 115), 15 to 17 minutes for medium (160°F; see page 115), or to the desired doneness. Remove and let sit for 5 minutes.

Coat the asparagus with the oil and season with salt and pepper. Grill over direct medium-high heat for 3 to 4 minutes. Cut the lamb into chops, and serve 2 per plate with the asparagus, garnished with the zest.

SERVES: 4

MARINADE AND LAMB
- 3/4 cup Dijon mustard
- 2 tablespoons honey
- 1/4 cup molasses
- 2 tablespoons dry vermouth or white wine
- 4 cloves garlic, minced
- 2 racks of lamb (8 ribs each, about 4 pounds total), trimmed of fat and cut in half

CRUST
- 1 1/2 cups toasted pine nuts
- 1/2 cup coarse breadcrumbs
- 3 tablespoons olive oil
- Salt and freshly ground black pepper to taste

ASPARAGUS
- 1 pound thin asparagus, trimmed
- 2 tablespoons olive oil
- Salt and freshly ground black pepper to taste
- 2 teaspoons grated lemon zest

The advantage of cooking cornbread on the grill is that it takes on smoky flavors, just like the campfire cornbread enjoyed by generations of cowboys on the range. The balsamic and port produce an irresistible sweet-and-tart combination.

Balsamic Vinegar & Port-Glazed Lamb
with Grilled Skillet Cornbread

CORNBREAD

2 small ears fresh sweet corn, husked

2 teaspoons olive oil

2 cups cornmeal

1 cup all-purpose flour

2 teaspoons salt

1/2 tablespoon baking powder

1 teaspoon baking soda

3 large eggs

1 cup buttermilk

1 cup half-and-half

1/2 cup melted butter, divided

2 red jalapeño chiles, seeded and minced

2 green jalapeño chiles, seeded and minced

3 tablespoons chopped cilantro

GLAZE AND LAMB

1 cup balsamic vinegar

1 cup port

1 tablespoon minced garlic

1/2 teaspoon salt

1/2 teaspoon freshly ground black pepper

8 bone-in lamb loin chops (about 5 ounces each and about 1 inch thick)

To prepare the cornbread, brush the corn with the oil and grill over indirect medium heat for 15 minutes, turning frequently, until lightly browned on all sides. Remove, and when cool enough to handle, cut the kernels from the cobs. Place the cornmeal, flour, salt, baking powder, and baking soda in a mixing bowl and mix well. In a separate bowl, whisk together the eggs, buttermilk, half-and-half, and all but 1 tablespoon of the butter, and pour into the cornmeal mixture. Fold in the grilled corn, chiles, and cilantro. Set a dry cast-iron skillet over high heat for 3 minutes to heat through. Add the remaining tablespoon of butter and heat for 1 minute. Pour in the batter and place the skillet on the grill over indirect medium heat. Cook for 30 to 35 minutes, or until golden brown and a toothpick inserted in the center comes out clean.

To prepare the glaze, place the vinegar, port, garlic, salt, and pepper in a saucepan and bring to a boil. Reduce the liquid by half over medium-high heat, about 10 minutes. Brush the lamb with the glaze and grill over direct medium-high heat for 4 minutes per side for medium-rare, 5 minutes per side for medium, or to the desired doneness, brushing with the glaze occasionally. Transfer to warm serving plates, spoon the warm glaze next to the chops, and serve with the cornbread.

SERVES: 4

Beer marinades are most often used for pork, but chicken also takes well to steeping in the "amber nectar," as our Australian friends call it. Since dark meat takes longer to grill than white meat, position the pieces accordingly and check frequently.

"Amber Nectar"
Drunken Chicken
with Grilled Zucchini

Place the beer, scallions, ginger, garlic, paprika, salt, pepper, parsley, and lemon juice in a mixing bowl and combine well. Place the chicken in a nonreactive baking dish and pour the marinade over. Let sit in the refrigerator for 4 or 5 hours or overnight, turning occasionally.

Place the zucchini on a platter, brush with the oil, and season with salt and pepper. Set aside.

Remove the chicken from the marinade and grill, skin-side down, over direct medium heat for 9 or 10 minutes. Turn over and repeat. To finish cooking, turn over and grill each piece of chicken for about 3 minutes longer on each side, or until the juices run clear. Meanwhile, grill the zucchini over direct medium-high heat for about 3 minutes on each side, or until tender. Transfer to serving plates and garnish with the lemon zest and wedges (for spritzing the zucchini). Serve with the chicken quarters.

SERVES: 4

MARINADE AND CHICKEN

- 3 cups (two 12-ounce bottles) amber ale or beer
- 2 scallions, sliced
- 2 teaspoons peeled and minced fresh ginger
- 2 teaspoons minced garlic
- 1 teaspoon paprika
- 1 teaspoon salt
- 1 teaspoon freshly ground pepper
- 1 tablespoon minced fresh parsley leaves
- 2 tablespoons freshly squeezed lemon juice (1 small lemon)
- 1 chicken (about 4 pounds), quartered

ZUCCHINI

- 8 small zucchini, cut in half lengthwise
- 2 tablespoons olive oil
- Salt and freshly ground black pepper to taste
- 1 tablespoon lemon zest for garnish
- 1 lemon, cut into 4 wedges

Green tomatillos, distant relatives of tomatoes (and, like them, native to Mexico), make a striking sauce; they can now be found in many supermarkets. For the most flavor, grill the chicken over fruit wood (or soaked chips) such as apple or cherry. Serve with rice.

Goat Cheese–Stuffed
Chicken Breast
with Blackened Tomatillo Sauce

CHICKEN AND STUFFING

4 large boneless chicken breasts (about 10 ounces each), skin on

3/4 cup goat cheese

1 tablespoon minced sun-dried tomatoes (packed in oil)

2 teaspoons minced fresh oregano leaves

Salt and freshly ground black pepper to taste

2 tablespoons olive oil

SAUCE

1 pound tomatillos, husked and rinsed

2 tablespoons olive oil

1 onion, chopped

2 cloves puréed grilled garlic (page 113) or minced fresh garlic

1/4 cup fresh cilantro leaves

2 jalapeño chiles, seeded and diced

1 teaspoon brown sugar

1 teaspoon salt

1/2 tablespoon freshly squeezed lime juice (1/2 medium lime)

To prepare the chicken, carefully make a slit along the side of each breast to form a large pocket. In a bowl, mix together the goat cheese, sun-dried tomatoes, and oregano, and season with salt and pepper. Stuff the chicken breasts with the mixture, securing horizontally with thin wooden skewers or toothpicks. Brush the chicken with olive oil and keep refrigerated until ready to grill.

To prepare the sauce, grill the tomatillos over direct medium heat, turning often, until the skins are partly blackened, about 10 to 12 minutes. Remove, coarsely chop, and transfer to a food processor. Heat the olive oil in a skillet and sauté the onion over medium-high heat for 5 minutes, until translucent. Transfer to the food processor and add the garlic, cilantro, jalapeños, sugar, and salt. Purée and transfer to a saucepan. Stir in the lime juice and warm through.

Grill the chicken over indirect medium heat (just off the direct heat), preferably using fruit wood or wood chips, skin side down, for about 10 minutes. Turn the breasts over, and cook over medium-high direct heat for about 8 minutes longer, or until cooked through. Spoon the warm sauce onto serving plates and place a chicken breast on top.

SERVES: 4

Buffalo wings with a difference! The Indian combination of curry spices and a cooling yogurt dip (called raita) is a similar formula to the American counterpart of hot sauce with blue-cheese dressing. If using whole wings, cut off the tips for stock.

Kashmiri Curried
Chicken Wings
with Minted Yogurt-Cucumber Dip

MARINADE AND CHICKEN

1 1/2 cups plain yogurt

1/4 cup peanut oil

1/2 tablespoon minced garlic

1/4 cup medium or mild curry powder

1 tablespoon ground cumin

1/2 tablespoon ground coriander

2 teaspoons pure red chile powder

3/4 teaspoon salt

20 chicken wings (4 to 4 1/2 pounds), rinsed and patted dry

DIP

1 cup plain yogurt

1 cup grated cucumber

1/4 cup minced fresh mint leaves

1/4 teaspoon salt

To prepare the wings, place the yogurt, oil, garlic, curry powder, cumin, coriander, chile powder, and salt in a mixing bowl. Cut the wings into 2 separate parts, add to the yogurt mixture, and coat well. Let sit in the refrigerator for 2 hours.

To prepare the dip, place the yogurt in a mixing bowl and stir in the cucumber, mint, and salt. Mix well, cover with plastic wrap, and refrigerate until ready to use.

Remove the wings from the marinade and scrape off any excess marinade. Grill over direct medium heat, turning often, for about 15 minutes, or until cooked through (when pierced with a knife, the skin near the bone should not appear pink). Serve the wings with the dip.

SERVES: 4

Cilantro is an integral part of Mexican, Southwestern, and many Asian cuisines. Its aromatic quality and the tang of citrus infuse the chicken, which pairs perfectly with the rich lushness of the salsa. Adding bell pepper to the salsa provides some crunch.

Cilantro-Garlic Marinated
Chicken Breast
with Avocado-Papaya Salsa

To prepare the marinade, place the cilantro, lemon juice, vinegar, onion, garlic, oregano, salt, pepper, and cumin in a blender and purée. Transfer to a mixing bowl and gradually whisk in the oil. Add the chicken and let marinate in the refrigerator for 2 hours, turning occasionally.

To prepare the salsa, place the avocados, papayas, bell pepper, scallions, and pepper flakes in a mixing bowl. In a separate bowl, whisk together the lime juice and olive oil and pour over the avocado mixture. Fold together gently to combine; season with salt. Serve at room temperature or chilled. Chill if not using immediately.

Remove the chicken from the marinade, draining off any excess liquid. Grill over direct medium-high heat for about 5 to 6 minutes per side, or until well cooked through. Transfer to serving plates and serve with the salsa.

SERVES: 4

MARINADE AND CHICKEN

1 cup chopped fresh cilantro leaves

3/4 cup freshly squeezed lemon juice (3 to 4 medium lemons)

6 tablespoons white wine vinegar

1/4 cup minced white onion

3 tablespoons minced garlic

1 tablespoon dried oregano

1/2 tablespoon salt

1/2 tablespoon freshly ground black pepper

1/2 tablespoon ground cumin

1 1/4 cups olive oil

8 boneless, skinless chicken breast halves (about 4 ounces each)

SALSA

2 avocados, peeled, pitted, and diced (about 2 cups)

2 small papayas, peeled, seeded, and diced (about 2 cups)

3 tablespoons diced red bell pepper

2 scallions, finely sliced

1/2 teaspoon red pepper flakes, or to taste

1 tablespoon freshly squeezed lime juice (1/2 large lime)

1 tablespoon olive oil

Salt to taste

This unusual and exotic presentation yields appetizer-size servings; for a main course, double the recipe and serve with rice. Lemongrass is a tall fibrous grass with lemony flavor; the best places to buy it fresh are at Southeast Asian markets.

Lemongrass-Speared Grilled
Chicken Satay
with Thai Peanut Sauce

Place the coconut milk, lime juice, oil, cilantro, ginger, sugar, and garlic in a mixing bowl and stir to dissolve the sugar. Cut each chicken breast lengthwise into 3 strips and let marinate in the refrigerator for 3 or 4 hours. Remove the outer leaves of each stalk of lemongrass and cut the thinner end at an angle to make lemongrass skewers; set aside.

To prepare the sauce, place the coconut milk, peanut butter, sugar, soy sauce, onion, curry paste, garlic, lemongrass, vinegar, lime zest, cilantro, and basil in a large saucepan. Bring just to a simmer while stirring, but do not boil. Continue cooking until the sauce thickens, about 15 minutes. Turn off the heat and strain the sauce before serving.

While the sauce is cooking, thread the marinated chicken strips onto the lemongrass skewers and grill over direct medium-high heat for 2 to 3 minutes per side, or until cooked through. Serve with the warm peanut sauce.

SERVES: 4

MARINADE AND CHICKEN

1/2 cup canned coconut milk

1/4 cup freshly squeezed lime juice (2 large limes)

1/4 cup peanut oil

2 tablespoons chopped fresh cilantro leaves

1 teaspoon peeled and minced fresh ginger

1 teaspoon sugar

1/2 teaspoon minced garlic

4 boneless, skinless chicken breast halves (about 4 ounces each)

4 lemongrass stalks (about 9 inches long)

SAUCE

1 1/2 cups canned coconut milk

6 tablespoons smooth peanut butter

3 tablespoons brown sugar

3 tablespoons soy sauce

3 tablespoons minced onion

2 tablespoons Thai red curry paste

1 tablespoon minced garlic

1 tablespoon minced fresh lemongrass

2 teaspoons unseasoned rice vinegar

1 teaspoon minced lime zest

1/2 cup minced fresh cilantro leaves

3 tablespoons minced fresh basil leaves

The rub and the brining technique, a traditional preparation for poultry and pork, produce a crispy skin, moist meat, and lots of flavor. If you prefer, use a mild chile powder or paprika. Grill the chicken and potatoes simultaneously.

Worcestershire & Chile-Rubbed
Whole Chicken
with Herbed Potatoes

CHICKEN AND RUB

- 1/2 cup salt, or 1 cup kosher salt
- 1 chicken (about 4 pounds)
- 1 tablespoon pure red chile powder
- 2 tablespoons Worcestershire sauce

POTATOES

- 1 1/2 pounds small Yukon Gold or yellow fingerling potatoes, scrubbed but unpeeled
- 3 cloves garlic, minced
- 3 tablespoons extra virgin olive oil
- 1 teaspoon dried marjoram or oregano
- Salt and freshly ground black pepper to taste
- 4 sprigs fresh marjoram or oregano for garnish

Mix the salt with 1 gallon water in a large mixing bowl or stock pot and add the chicken, breast side down. Let sit in the refrigerator overnight.

Remove the chicken from the brine, pat dry, and transfer to a platter. Sprinkle the chile powder all over the chicken and gradually pour over the Worcestershire sauce, spreading the moist rub all over the skin with your hand.

Grill the chicken breast-side up over indirect medium to medium-high heat, placing a drip pan beneath the chicken. Cover the grill, vent it slightly, and cook for 65 to 75 minutes, or until the internal temperature reaches 170°F (see page 115) and the juices run clear; the skin should be browned and crispy. Occasionally baste the skin with a little more Worcestershire sauce while cooking. Remove from the grill and let rest for 7 or 8 minutes before carving.

Place the potatoes in a roasting pan and add the garlic, oil, dried marjoram, salt, and pepper. Coat the potatoes and place the pan on the covered grill over indirect heat. Grill for about 1 hour, stirring occasionally, or until tender.

Carve the chicken, serve with the potatoes, and garnish each plate with a marjoram sprig.
SERVES: 4

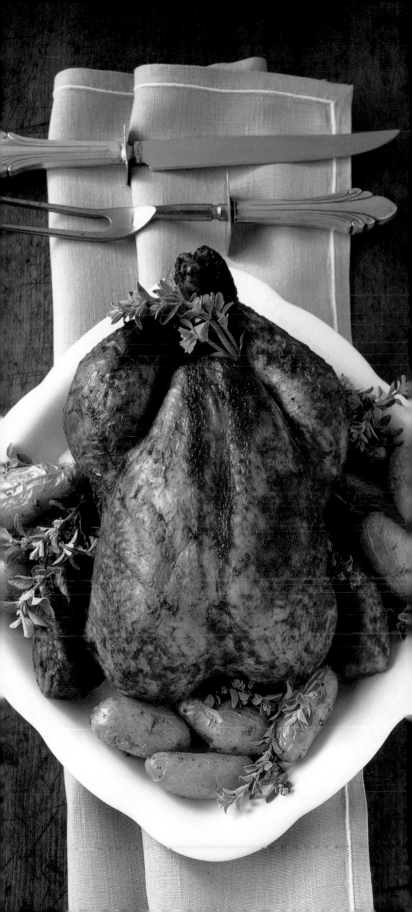

Honey and mustard make a classic sweet-and-hot combination. Whenever you use a glaze containing any type of sugar, grill over a medium fire (as here) to prevent burning. The potatoes make a good all-purpose side for many grilled foods.

Home-Style
Honey-Mustard Chicken
with Grilled Garlicky Potatoes

POTATOES

1 1/2 pounds new potatoes

3 tablespoons olive oil, divided

1 teaspoon puréed grilled garlic (page 113) or minced fresh garlic

1 tablespoon minced fresh mint leaves (optional)

Kosher salt or sea salt to taste

CHICKEN AND SAUCE

8 boneless, skinless chicken breast halves (about 4 ounces each)

Salt and freshly ground black pepper to taste

3 tablespoons honey

3 tablespoons Dijon mustard

2 tablespoons freshly squeezed lemon juice (1 small lemon)

2 tablespoons white wine vinegar

1/2 cup peanut oil

Cut the potatoes in half and place in a mixing bowl. Pour half of the oil over the potatoes and mix to coat. Using a grilling vegetable basket, grill over medium-high heat for 12 to 15 minutes, or until tender, turning frequently. Transfer to the mixing bowl and toss with the remaining oil, the garlic, mint, and salt. Keep warm.

Meanwhile, season the chicken breasts with salt and pepper and set aside. In a bowl, combine the honey, mustard, lemon juice, and vinegar. Gradually whisk in the oil until completely incorporated. Set aside 1/2 cup for drizzling at the end. Brush the chicken with the remaining mixture and grill over direct medium heat for 5 to 6 minutes per side, or until well cooked through, brushing again just before and after turning. Transfer to warm serving plates and serve with the potatoes. Drizzle the reserved 1/2 cup of honey-mustard mixture over the chicken before serving.

SERVES: 4

Jim is executive chef at Philadephia's acclaimed Rittenhouse Hotel. For more of Jim's heart-healthy recipes, pick up his masterpiece, The Rittenhouse Cookbook. For this slightly adapted recipe, you can substitute yellow tortillas for the blue ones.

Jim Coleman's Grilled Chicken
Peppery Salad
with Melon Salsa

To prepare the salsa, place both types of melon, the chile, onion, lime juice, cilantro, and mint in a mixing bowl and keep chilled.

Preheat the oven to 325°F. To prepare the salad, lightly coat a baking sheet with nonstick cooking spray (or a little vegetable oil) and place the tortilla strips in a single layer on the sheet. Bake in the oven for 20 minutes, or until golden brown. Remove from the oven and let cool. Place the arugula and mesclun greens in a mixing bowl and toss gently but thoroughly with the lemon juice. Set aside.

Lightly brush the chicken with the oil and season with salt and pepper. Grill over direct medium-high heat for about 5 minutes per side, or until cooked through.

To serve, place some of the salad in a strip down one side of each serving plate. Arrange the salsa on the opposite side of each plate. Slice each chicken breast and place on top of the salad. Garnish the chicken by placing a tortilla strip upright between each slice of chicken and serve immediately.

SERVES: 4

SALSA
- 3/4 cup diced cantaloupe
- 3/4 cup diced honeydew
- 1 jalapeño chile, seeded and thinly sliced
- 3 tablespoons finely diced red onion
- 2 teaspoons freshly squeezed lime juice (1/2 medium lime)
- 1 teaspoon chopped fresh cilantro leaves
- 1 teaspoon chopped fresh mint leaves

SALAD AND CHICKEN
- 2 yellow corn tortillas, cut into 1/2-inch-thick strips (or tall triangles)
- 2 blue corn tortillas, cut into 1/2 inch thick strips (or tall triangles)
- 3 ounces arugula or mizuna lettuce (about 2 1/2 cups)
- 3 ounces mesclun greens (about 2 1/2 cups)
- Juice of 3 lemons
- 4 boneless, skinless chicken breast halves (about 5 ounces each)
- 1 tablespoon vegetable oil
- Salt and freshly ground black pepper to taste

Jerk, the fiery Jamaican seasoning mix, is typically used for grilled or barbecued chicken and pork, and the Trelawny Parish area produces some of the best. If habaneros or Scotch bonnets (probably the hottest of all) are unavailable, use 2 tablespoons hot chile sauce.

Trelawny Parish Jamaican
Jerk Chicken
with Red Chile Grilled Corn

Place all the jerk ingredients except the chicken in the bowl of a food processor and purée until smooth. Place the chicken in a mixing bowl, cover with the jerk paste, and refrigerate for at least 4 hours, turning occasionally.

Place the corn in a large bowl of warm water and soak for 1 hour. Meanwhile, place the butter, lime juice, chile powder, paprika, and salt in a shallow bowl and mix well. Peel the corn husks back and generously spread the butter mixture over the corn kernels. Fold the husks over the kernels and grill over direct medium-high heat for about 20 to 25 minutes, turning occasionally.

While the corn is grilling, remove the chicken from the refrigerator, leaving on as much of the jerk paste as possible. Grill over direct medium heat for about 30 minutes, turning often, or until the chicken is cooked through and the juices run clear. Transfer to warm serving plates. Unwrap the corn and serve with the chicken.

SERVES: 4

JERK PASTE AND CHICKEN

- 3/4 cup chopped red onion
- 1/4 cup freshly squeezed lime juice (2 large limes)
- 1/4 cup sliced scallions
- 2 tablespoons peeled and minced fresh ginger
- 2 tablespoons soy sauce
- 2 tablespoons olive oil
- 1 tablespoon honey
- 1 tablespoon chopped garlic
- 2 teaspoons minced fresh thyme leaves
- 3 tablespoons ground allspice
- 1/2 tablespoon salt
- 1 teaspoon ground cinnamon
- 1 teaspoon freshly ground black pepper
- 1/2 teaspoon ground nutmeg
- 3 habanero or Scotch bonnet chiles, seeded and chopped, or to taste
- 1 chicken (about 4 pounds), cut into 4 bone-in pieces

CORN

- 4 ears fresh sweet corn, husks attached and silks removed
- 1/2 cup unsalted butter, at room temperature
- 1 tablespoon freshly squeezed lime juice (1/2 large lime)
- 1 tablespoon pure red chile powder
- 1 teaspoon paprika
- 1 teaspoon salt

Tuna types include bluefin, albacore, and yellowfin—called ahi in Hawaii—which is most favored for sushi and sashimi because of its flavor. For a shortcut, use 2 or 3 tablespoons of a medium-hot chile sauce instead of the rehydrated anchos.

Grilled
Yellowfin Tuna
with Ancho Chile-Orange Sauce

SAUCE

4 dried ancho chiles, stemmed and seeded

4 cups hot water

3 cloves garlic, chopped

2 cups freshly squeezed orange juice (4 to 5 large oranges)

6 tablespoons freshly squeezed lime juice (4 medium limes)

1/2 teaspoon ground allspice

1/2 teaspoon salt

2 tablespoons olive oil

2 tablespoons freshly squeezed lime juice (1 large lime)

16 scallions, trimmed (to about 6 or 7 inches long)

FISH

4 high-quality, center-cut yellowfin or albacore tuna steaks (about 8 ounces each and 1 inch thick)

2 tablespoons peanut oil

Salt and freshly ground white pepper to taste

1 teaspoon paprika

To prepare the sauce, place the anchos in a hot, dry skillet and toast over medium heat for 3 minutes, shaking the pan often. Place the hot water in a bowl, add the anchos, and let rehydrate for 25 minutes, until soft. Remove the chiles with tongs and transfer to a blender. Add 1/2 cup of the soaking liquid, the garlic, orange juice, lime juice, allspice, and salt. Purée, then strain into a saucepan and bring to a boil. Turn down the heat and simmer for 15 minutes.

Place the olive oil and lime juice in a bowl, stir together, and marinate the scallions while preparing the fish. Place the tuna on a platter and cover with the oil. Make sure both sides of the fish are coated, and season with salt, pepper, and paprika. Lightly oil the cooking grate of the hot grill with a long-handled brush. Grill the tuna over direct medium-high heat for 2 to 3 minutes per side for medium-rare, about 4 to 5 minutes for medium, or to the desired doneness, turning only once. Grill the scallions until just wilted, about 2 minutes. Arrange 4 of the scallions in a square on each warm serving plate and spoon some of the warm sauce inside the scallions. Place the tuna on the sauce and serve.

SERVES: 4

Salmon and dill make a classic combination, as Scandinavian gravlax proves. Take care not to overcook salmon. Alder is a good match, but any fruit or nut wood (or chips) can be used. You can dispense with the wine marinade and drizzle with a little oil instead.

Alder-Grilled
Salmon Steaks
with Creamy Dill Sauce

Place the wine, oil, lemon juice, garlic, salt, and pepper in a nonreactive baking dish and whisk together. Add the salmon and let sit for 30 minutes, turning occasionally.

Meanwhile, to prepare the sauce, place the dill, vinegar, salt, pepper, and mustard in a saucepan. Stir in the sour cream and milk and heat until warm; do not boil. (Alternatively, the sauce can be served cold, if you prefer.)

Remove the salmon from the marinade, draining any excess liquid. Using alder wood or wood chips (or any fruit wood), grill the salmon over direct medium-high heat for about 5 minutes per side, or until cooked through, turning gently only once. Transfer the salmon to serving plates and spoon the sauce around it.

SERVES: 4

MARINADE AND FISH

- $1/2$ cup white wine
- $1/4$ cup olive oil
- 2 tablespoons freshly squeezed lemon juice (1 small lemon)
- 2 cloves garlic, minced
- Salt and freshly ground black pepper to taste
- 4 salmon steaks (about 8 ounces each and about 1 inch thick)

DILL SAUCE

- 3 tablespoons minced fresh dill weed, or 2 teaspoons dried
- 1 tablespoon white wine vinegar
- Salt and freshly ground black pepper
- 1 tablespoon Dijon mustard
- 1 cup sour cream
- $1 1/2$ tablespoons milk

Red snapper should not be confused with the unrelated rockfish, which is sometimes erroneously marketed as snapper. In addition to superior flavor and texture, red snapper has an intense pink-red skin while rockfish is paler and has a bony-looking face.

Grilled Whole
Red Snapper
with Grilled Vegetables in Yellow Peppers

VEGETABLES

- 1/2 cup olive oil
- 2 tablespoons balsamic vinegar
- Salt and freshly ground black pepper to taste
- 2 red or yellow bell peppers, stems left on, cut in half lengthwise and seeded
- 20 asparagus spears
- 4 cherry tomatoes
- 1 ear sweet corn, husked
- 8 chanterelle or shiitake mushrooms

FISH

- 4 whole red snappers (1 to 1 1/2 pounds each), fins trimmed, scaled, and gutted
- 1/4 cup vegetable oil
- 2 teaspoons paprika
- 1/2 teaspoon salt
- 4 lemon wedges

To prepare the vegetables, place the oil, balsamic vinegar, salt, and pepper in a mixing bowl. Brush the peppers, asparagus, tomatoes, corn, and mushrooms with the mixture. Thread the cherry tomatoes on 2 parallel skewers. Grill the peppers, asparagus, tomatoes, and corn over direct medium heat for 7 to 10 minutes, turning occasionally, until each vegetable is al dente; do not overcook. Grill the mushrooms for 2 to 3 minutes and set aside. Cut the top 2 to 3 inches of the asparagus spears (use the rest for soup or stock), remove the cherry tomatoes from the skewers and cut in half, and cut the kernels from the corn when cool enough to handle. Arrange a bell pepper half on each serving plate with the grilled vegetables inside; place any excess vegetables on the plate next to the peppers.

Score the sides of each fish with 3 diagonal slashes about 1/2 inch deep. Brush the fish with the oil and sprinkle with the paprika and salt. Place in a fish grill basket and grill the snapper over direct medium-high heat for 8 to 10 minutes per side, or until cooked through and opaque, turning gently only once. Transfer to serving plates, arrange the lemon wedges next to the fish for spritzing, and serve with the vegetables. Garnish the plate with the grilled mushrooms.

SERVES: 4

Of all fish, tuna probably has a texture most like red meat, and is readily available in steaks that are reminiscent of a filet mignon. This combination of flavors and ingredients is typical of the contemporary "Hawaii Regional Cuisine."

Seared Ginger-Soy
Marinated Tuna
with Soy-Mustard Sauce

MARINADE AND FISH

- 1 cup soy sauce
- 1/2 cup dry sherry
- 3 tablespoons brown sugar
- 2 tablespoons peeled and minced fresh ginger
- 1 tablespoon minced garlic
- 3 scallions, finely sliced
- 4 high-quality center-cut bluefin or yellowfin tuna steaks (about 8 ounces each and 1 inch thick)

SAUCE

- 1 tablespoon hot water
- 2 tablespoons dry mustard (such as Colman's)
- 2 tablespoons soy sauce
- 1/2 cup white wine
- 1 tablespoon white wine vinegar
- 1/2 tablespoon freshly squeezed lemon juice (1/2 small lemon)
- 1 tablespoon minced shallots
- 3 tablespoons heavy cream
- 1/2 cup unsalted butter, diced

GARNISH

- 1 teaspoon black sesame seeds for garnish
- 1 tablespoon pickled ginger for garnish

To prepare the marinade, place the soy sauce, sherry, sugar, ginger, garlic, and scallions in a mixing bowl or nonreactive baking dish. Add the tuna and marinate in the refrigerator for 1 hour, turning occasionally if not covered by the marinade.

Meanwhile, prepare the sauce. Pour the hot water into a bowl; add the mustard and mix to form a paste. Stir in the soy sauce and let sit for 10 minutes. Place the wine, vinegar, lemon juice, and shallots in a saucepan and bring to a boil. Reduce the liquid over medium-high heat until syrupy and about 3 tablespoons of liquid remain. Add the cream and reduce the mixture by half. Turn down the heat to low and add the butter, a little at a time, and stir until each piece is incorporated; do not to let the mixture boil or it will separate. Strain through a fine sieve into a clean saucepan. Gradually stir in the mustard-soy mixture and keep warm.

Lightly oil the cooking grate of the hot grill with a long-handled brush. Grill the tuna over direct medium-high heat for about 3 minutes per side for medium-rare, 4 to 5 minutes for medium, or to the desired doneness, turning only once. Serve with the sauce, and garnish with the sesame seeds and pickled ginger.

SERVES: 4

Mahimahi, a firm-fleshed, moistly textured, warm-water fish (also called dolphin fish or dorado), is one of the most colorful fish in the water. The spicy Provençal-style flavored mayonnaise and fish are great with crispy onions (see page 48).

Seared
Mahimahi
Sandwich, North-Shore Style

To prepare the spread, place the mustard, garlic, egg and yolk, and lemon juice in a blender and purée. With the machine running, gradually add the olive oil until incorporated. Season with the salt, chile powder, and paprika; combine thoroughly. Thin with a little water if necessary. Refrigerate.

Place the mahimahi filets on a platter and pour the oil over. Make sure both sides of the fish are coated, and season with salt and pepper. Lightly oil the cooking grate of the hot grill with a long-handled brush. Grill the fish over direct medium-high heat for 4 to 5 minutes per side, or to the desired doneness, turning only once.

While the fish is grilling, toast the rolls on the grill. Transfer to serving plates and spread each half with ½ tablespoon of the aïoli. Divide the lettuce leaves between the rolls and top with the tomato, if desired, and the grilled mahimahi.

SERVES: 4

Note: Uncooked eggs are not recommended for immuno-compromised individuals or small children. As an alternative in the recipe for the aïoli spread, simply add the chile powder to a commercial mayonnaise.

SPICY AÏOLI SPREAD

- 2 teaspoons Dijon mustard
- 1 teaspoon minced garlic
- 1 large egg plus 1 large egg yolk
- 1 tablespoon freshly squeezed lemon juice (½ small lemon)
- 1 cup olive oil
- Pinch of salt
- 1 teaspoon red chile powder
- 1 teaspoon paprika

SANDWICHES

- 4 skinless mahimahi filets (about 6 to 7 ounces each)
- 2 tablespoons peanut oil
- Salt and freshly ground black pepper to taste
- 4 crusty poppy seed or kaiser rolls, split in half
- 12 to 16 Boston or Bibb lettuce leaves
- 4 thin slices vine-ripened tomato (optional)

The meaty, moderately fat flesh of swordfish makes it ideal for grilling. Unlike tuna, it should be cooked through, but is tough and dry if overcooked. The flavorful sauce makes a striking contrast to both the grilled exterior and the white meat inside.

Grilled Zested
Swordfish
with Red Bell Pepper–Plum Tomato Sauce

To prepare the fish, mix together the lemon zest, black pepper, paprika, garlic salt, tarragon, cayenne, and oil in a nonreactive baking dish. Add the swordfish and rub with the mixture, making sure both sides of the fish are covered. Let sit in the refrigerator for 30 minutes to 1 hour.

Meanwhile, prepare the sauce. Roast the bell peppers on the grill and let steam (see page 113 to 114). When cool, peel, seed, dice, and set aside. Heat the olive oil in a saucepan and sauté the onion over medium-high heat for 3 to 4 minutes. Add the bell peppers, garlic, tomatoes, thyme, honey, salt, and pepper. Turn down the heat to medium-low, cover the pan, and cook for 15 to 20 minutes. Transfer to a blender or food processor and purée until smooth. Transfer to a clean saucepan and keep warm.

Oil the cooking grate of the hot grill with a long-handled brush. Grill the swordfish over direct medium-high heat for 5 to 6 minutes per side, or until cooked through and opaque, turning gently only once. Transfer to serving plates and serve with the sauce.

SERVES: 4

ZEST RUB AND FISH

- 1 tablespoon minced lemon zest
- 2 teaspoons freshly ground black pepper
- 2 teaspoons paprika
- 1 teaspoon garlic salt
- 1 teaspoon dried tarragon
- $1/2$ teaspoon cayenne
- $1/4$ cup olive oil
- 4 swordfish filets (7 or 8 ounces each and 1 inch thick)

SAUCE

- 3 red bell peppers
- 2 tablespoons olive oil
- 1 onion, finely diced
- 2 cloves garlic, minced
- 4 plum tomatoes, blanched, peeled, seeded, and diced (page 114)
- $1/2$ teaspoon minced fresh thyme leaves
- $1/2$ tablespoon honey
- Salt and freshly ground black pepper to taste

Marinating—or sousing—and glazing fish with rum
have been popularized by the "New World Cuisine"
of southern Florida that borrows from the Caribbean
and Central and South America. This fish and salsa will
certainly put you in a tropical frame of mind.

Rum-Soused &
Rum-Glazed Halibut
with Tropical Fruit Salsa

SOUSE AND FISH

1 cup white rum

1/4 cup olive oil

3 tablespoons white wine
vinegar

3 cloves garlic, minced

1 teaspoon ground
cinnamon

2 tablespoons brown
sugar

1 teaspoon vanilla extract

Salt and freshly ground
white pepper to taste

4 halibut or sea bass
filets (7 or 8 ounces
each and about
1 inch thick)

1 teaspoon hot chile
sauce, or to taste

SALSA

1 mango, peeled, pitted,
and diced

1 papaya (preferably
pink-fleshed), cut in
half, seeded, peeled,
and diced

1/3 pineapple, cored,
peeled, and diced

2 kiwi fruit, peeled
and diced

1/2 red bell pepper,
seeded and diced

Juice of 1/2 lime

To prepare the souse, place the rum, oil, vinegar, garlic, cinnamon, brown sugar, vanilla, salt, and pepper in a baking dish or shallow bowl. Add the halibut and marinate in the refrigerator for 30 minutes, turning occasionally.

Meanwhile, prepare the salsa. Place the mango, papaya, pineapple, kiwi fruit, bell pepper, and lime juice in a bowl and keep refrigerated.

Remove the fish from the souse and set aside on a plate. Transfer the souse to a saucepan, add the chile sauce, and bring to a boil. Turn down the heat and simmer until the mixture thickens, about 5 minutes. Remove from the heat.

Lightly oil the cooking grate of the hot grill with a long-handled brush. Grill the halibut over direct medium-high heat for about 5 minutes per side, or until cooked through and opaque, turning gently only once. Brush with the glaze frequently. Serve with the salsa.
SERVES: 4

Mignonette sauce is traditional for raw oysters, and here we add bell peppers for color, texture, and flavor. Serve with small oyster forks and teaspoons, and for a striking presentation, arrange on a platter lined with a mixture of rock salt and peppercorns.

Mesquite-Grilled
Oysters
with Bell Pepper Mignonette

To prepare the mignonette, place the lemon juice, shallots, bell peppers, black pepper, and Tabasco in a bowl and thoroughly combine.

Prepare the grill using mesquite charcoal, mesquite wood, or soaked mesquite chips. Place the oysters over direct medium-high heat and grill for 5 or 6 minutes, until they have opened; remove from the grill as soon as they open and discard any that do not open. Reserve both halves of the oyster shells.

Place the rock salt on 4 serving plates and place both halves of 6 oysters on each plate. Spoon a little of the mignonette over each oyster, and spoon the rest into the empty halves of each shell. Garnish each plate with a lemon wedge (for spritzing the oysters).

SERVES: 4

MIGNONETTE

- 1/2 cup freshly squeezed lemon juice (2 to 3 medium lemons)
- 1/4 cup minced shallots
- 1/4 cup very finely diced red bell pepper
- 1/4 cup very finely diced yellow bell pepper
- 1/4 cup very finely diced green bell pepper
- 1 teaspoon freshly ground black pepper
- 1 teaspoon Tabasco sauce (optional)

OYSTERS

- 2 dozen large fresh oysters, scrubbed
- 2 pounds rock salt
- 1 lemon cut into 4 wedges

You will be convinced that you're lying in a hammock on some palm-fringed shore in Mexico's Yucatán peninsula. As the grilling aroma rises and the sun sparkles on the turquoise sea, you raise your margarita glass to your sociable company and to the good life.

Tequila-Marinated
Grilled Shrimp
and Pineapple Skewers with Papaya Relish

RELISH

2 papayas, seeded, peeled, and diced

1 red onion, finely diced

1 small Asian pear, or 2 Bosc pears, peeled, cored, and finely diced

2 canned chipotle chiles in adobo sauce, minced

1/4 cup sugar

1/4 cup water

3 tablespoons apple cider vinegar

MARINADE, SHRIMP, AND PINEAPPLE

Juice and zest of 6 limes

Juice and zest of 4 oranges

1 teaspoon minced garlic

1/2 cup good-quality tequila (such as Herradura silver)

1/2 cup unseasoned rice wine vinegar

2 teaspoons dried red pepper flakes (optional)

1 1/2 pounds jumbo shrimp, peeled, deveined, washed, and patted dry

1 1/2 cups fresh pineapple cut into 1-inch cubes

To prepare the relish, place half of the papayas, the onion, pear, chiles, sugar, water, and vinegar in a saucepan and bring to a boil, stirring often. Turn down the heat to a simmer and cook for 40 minutes, stirring occasionally. Transfer to a mixing bowl and add the remaining papaya. Let cool.

While the relish is cooling, prepare the marinade. Place the citrus juices and zests, garlic, tequila, vinegar, and pepper flakes in a mixing bowl and add the shrimp and pineapple. Let marinate in the refrigerator for 30 minutes (do not marinate any longer or the shrimp will "cook" in the marinade).

Remove the shrimp and pineapple from the marinade and thread onto 8 bamboo skewers that have been soaked in water for 30 minutes or metal skewers. (If possible, use 16 skewers: place the shrimp and pineapple on 2 parallel skewers to keep them from spinning around and cooking unevenly.) Grill the skewers over direct high heat for 2 to 3 minutes per side, or until the shrimp are cooked through and pink all over.

Place 2 skewers on each plate and serve with the relish.
SERVES: 4

We recommend cold-water lobster tails from New Zealand, Australia, and South Africa, or you may substitute the warm-water variety from Brazil and the Caribbean. Serve with a crusty bread and grilled corn or asparagus.

Grilled Rock
Lobster Tails
with Red Chile Butter Dipping Sauce

Place ¼ cup of the butter and 1 tablespoon of the lemon juice in a bowl and whisk together. Using scissors, cut the membrane covering the underside of the tails and remove. Cut the meat and shell of each tail in half lengthwise with a sharp heavy knife. Brush the butter mixture over the lobster meat. Grill shell-side down over direct high heat for 3 minutes, or until the shell turns pink, brushing the meat once or twice with the butter mixture. Turn the tails over and grill for about 2 minutes longer. Turn the tails shell-side down again, brush once more with the butter, and grill for 1 minute more.

Place the remaining ¾ cup of butter, the remaining 2 tablespoons of lemon juice, the garlic, cayenne, salt, and pepper in a separate mixing bowl, and whisk together. Pour the mixture into 4 small ramekins and serve with the grilled lobster tails.

SERVES: 4

- 1 cup clarified butter, divided
- 3 tablespoons freshly squeezed lemon juice (1 medium lemon), divided
- 4 uncooked rock lobster tails (6 or 7 ounces each)
- ½ teaspoon puréed grilled garlic (page 113) or fresh garlic mashed to a paste
- ½ teaspoon cayenne or paprika
- Salt and freshly ground white pepper to taste

Scallops are usually shelled at sea, so may not be the freshest in stores. If possible, purchase loose so you can smell them, and don't buy if they have an ammonia-like aroma. They should not be floating in liquid (a preservative), and they should feel firm.

Orangey-Garlic
Sea Scallops
with Zesty Black Bean Sauce

SAUCE

1 tablespoon olive oil

3 slices bacon, diced

1 teaspoon minced garlic

1 small onion, diced

1 stick celery, sliced

1 carrot, sliced

1 small red bell pepper, seeded and diced

2 jalapeño chiles, seeded and minced

1 teaspoon ground cumin

1 can (15 ounces) cooked black beans

1/4 cup sherry vinegar or white wine vinegar

2 tablespoons freshly squeezed orange juice (1/2 small orange)

1 teaspoon minced orange zest

1 cup chicken stock

Salt and freshly ground black pepper to taste

SCALLOPS AND MARINADE

1 1/2 pounds sea scallops (about 25 to 30)

1/4 cup olive oil

6 tablespoons freshly squeezed orange juice (1 medium orange)

1 teaspoon minced fresh garlic

1/2 teaspoon freshly ground white pepper

2 teaspoons orange zest cut in very thin strips for garnish

To prepare the sauce, heat the olive oil in a saucepan and add the bacon. Sauté over medium-high heat for 3 minutes. Add the garlic and onion and cook for 2 minutes longer. Add the celery, carrot, bell pepper, and jalapeños, and cook for 10 minutes, until completely soft. Add the cumin, beans, vinegar, orange juice, orange zest, and stock and bring to a boil. Turn down the heat and simmer for 10 minutes. Transfer to a blender and purée. Return to a clean saucepan, season with salt and pepper, and keep warm.

To prepare the scallops, wash, pat dry, and place in a mixing bowl. In another bowl, whisk together the oil, orange juice, garlic, and pepper. Pour over the scallops and marinate in the refrigerator for 30 minutes (do not marinate any longer or the scallops will "cook" in the orange juice). Turn the scallops once. Remove from the marinade, drain any excess liquid, and grill over direct high heat for 1 to 2 minutes per side, or until opaque; brush with the marinade as they cook.

Spoon the sauce onto 4 warm serving plates. Serve the scallops in a circle on top of the sauce and garnish with the orange zest.

SERVES: 4

Not long ago, the choice was domestic (or button) mushrooms or those hunted yourself in the wild, but now there is an array of wild and cultivated varieties. The thick, rich texture of the giant portobello seems like meat, and the flavors here are irresistible.

Grilled Portobello Mushroom & Red Bell Pepper Sandwich
with Spicy Aïoli

Grill the bell peppers over direct medium-high heat, remove, and let steam (see page 113 to 114). When cool, peel, seed, and cut into halves. Set aside. Meanwhile, place the oil, balsamic vinegar, garlic, salt, and pepper in a mixing bowl. Brush the mushrooms on both sides with the oil and transfer to the bowl. Toss gently to coat the mushrooms, and let sit for 10 minutes.

Grill the mushrooms over direct medium-high heat for 4 to 5 minutes per side, or until moist and tender when pierced with a knife. Let cool slightly. Lightly toast the rolls on the grill, transfer to serving plates, and spread each half with ½ tablespoon of the aïoli. Place 2 lettuce leaves on the bottom half of each roll, add a grilled mushroom, and top with a tomato slice, a bell pepper half, 3 basil leaves, and the top of each roll.

SERVES: 4

MUSHROOMS AND BELL PEPPERS

- 2 red bell peppers
- 1/4 cup olive oil
- 2 tablespoons balsamic vinegar
- 1/2 teaspoon minced garlic
- Salt and freshly ground black pepper to taste
- 4 portobello mushrooms (about 4 ounces each), stemmed and cleaned

SANDWICHES

- 4 poppy seed rolls, kaiser rolls, or baps
- 1/2 cup Spicy Aïoli Spread (page 91)
- 8 leaves Bibb or Boston lettuce
- 4 large slices tomato
- 12 fresh basil leaves

Grilling makes an interesting and flavorful alternative to oven-cooked pizzas. For a rustic effect, roll out the dough in a circle but do not attempt to trim it into an exactly round shape. For a short-cut, use a commercial ready-to-go pizza crust.

Tomato & Shiitake Mushroom
Grilled Pizza

PIZZA DOUGH

- 3/4 cup lukewarm water (110°F)
- 1/2 package active dry yeast
- 1 tablespoon honey
- 2 cups all-purpose flour
- 1/4 teaspoon salt
- 2 tablespoons olive oil

TOPPING

- 1 pound plum tomatoes
- Salt and freshly ground black pepper to taste
- 3 tablespoons olive oil, divided
- 20 shiitake mushroom caps, chopped
- 4 teaspoons puréed grilled garlic (page 113)
- 1 cup shredded mozzarella cheese
- 1 tablespoon julienned fresh basil leaves
- 1 tablespoon grated Parmesan cheese

To prepare the dough, pour the water in a mixing bowl and sprinkle in the yeast. Whisk in the honey and let sit in a warm place for 5 minutes. Sift the flour and salt into a large mixing bowl, stir in the liquid mixture, and mix until a soft dough forms. Add the oil and continue to mix until the dough becomes shiny and forms a ball. Turn out onto a floured work surface and knead for 8 to 10 minutes, or until smooth; add a little more flour if necessary. Transfer the dough to a lightly oiled bowl, cover with a damp towel or plastic wrap, and let rise in a warm place for 45 minutes, or until doubled in volume. Return to a lightly floured work surface and divide into 4 portions. Knead each portion for 1 minute and form into balls. Place on a baking sheet, cover again, and let rise for 20 minutes. Roll each ball into 6-inch circles about 1/8 inch thick, sprinkling the dough and rolling pin with additional flour to prevent them from sticking. Pinch the edges of the dough to create a raised brim. Set aside.

While the dough is rising, grill the tomatoes over direct medium-high heat, turning often, until the skins are somewhat cracked and partly blackened, about 10 minutes. Remove the seeds, roughly chop, and season with salt and pepper. Heat 2 tablespoons of the oil in a sauté pan and sauté the shiitake mushrooms over medium-high heat for 2 to 3 minutes, until softened. Grill the dough over direct high heat, covered, for about 1 minute, until the

bottom side hardens. Remove from the grill and brush the grilled sides with the remaining 1 tablespoon of the oil and the grilled garlic. Add the tomatoes and sprinkle with the mozzarella and mushrooms, making sure that some of the grill marks show around the outside. Grill, covered, for 3 or 4 minutes, until the cheese has melted. Garnish with the basil and sprinkle the Parmesan over the pizzas.

SERVES: 4

This is a simple salad that pairs a classic combo—mild new potatoes and slightly sweet mint—with peppery watercress. Use arugula, mizuna lettuce, or any other strongly flavored green instead of the watercress, if you wish, or a mesclun salad mix.

Grilled Potato &
Watercress Salad
with Mint Vinaigrette

POTATOES

- 1 1/2 pounds new potatoes, cut in half
- 3 tablespoons olive oil
- 1 teaspoon minced fresh garlic
- 1 teaspoon minced fresh mint leaves
- 1 teaspoon freshly squeezed lemon juice (1/2 small lemon)
- Salt and freshly ground black pepper to taste

VINAIGRETTE AND SALAD

- 1/4 cup chopped fresh mint leaves
- 2 tablespoons apple cider vinegar
- 1 tablespoon freshly squeezed lemon juice (1/2 small lemon)
- 1/2 teaspoon sugar
- 1/4 teaspoon salt
- 5 tablespoons extra virgin olive oil
- 4 ounces watercress leaves

Place the potatoes in a roasting pan and add the oil, garlic, 1 teaspoon mint, lemon juice, salt, and pepper. Mix well and place on the covered grill over indirect heat. Grill for 40 to 50 minutes, stirring occasionally, or until tender.

Meanwhile, for the vinaigrette, place the 1/4 cup chopped mint, the vinegar, lemon juice, sugar, and salt in a blender or food processor and purée. Gradually add the oil in a steady stream, until completely incorporated.

Arrange the watercress on serving plates and top with the potatoes. Drizzle the vinaigrette over and serve.

SERVES: 4

Here is an old standby that's been updated a little with sun-dried tomatoes and grilled peppers, then given the benefit of grilling. For those without cholesterol worries, brush the slices with melted butter instead of the oil for a richer flavor.

The Nouveau
Grilled Cheese
Sandwich with Red Bell Peppers

Grill the bell peppers over direct medium-high heat, remove, and let steam (see page 113 to 114). When cool, peel, seed, and cut into halves. Brush one side of each slice of bread with the oil; place oil-side down on a platter. Place a slice of cheese on 4 slices of the bread, and top with the sun-dried tomatoes. Add another slice of cheese, and then a bell pepper half. Season with salt and pepper, and top with the remaining slices of bread, oil-sides up.

Transfer to the grill and cook over direct medium-high heat for 2 minutes on each side, or until the bread is slightly browned and the cheese is melting. Remove to serving plates and cut each sandwich in half on a diagonal.

SERVES: 4

2 large red bell peppers
8 slices multigrain bread
1/4 cup extra virgin olive oil
8 slices Swiss or mozzarella cheese
16 sun-dried tomatoes (packed in oil), drained and chopped
Salt and freshly ground black pepper to taste

This wonderful medley is from chef Stephan Pyles, whose restaurants include Star Canyon, AquaKnox, and Canoñita in Dallas and Las Vegas. Stephan is the author of Southwestern Vegetarian (Clarkson Potter), a beautiful companion to his acclaimed PBS television series.

Stephan's Grilled Summer Vegetables
with Lemon Zest Aïoli

AÏOLI

2 cups mayonnaise

1/4 cup puréed grilled garlic (page 113)

2 tablespoons minced lemon zest (4 or 5 lemons)

VEGETABLES

3 tablespoons freshly squeezed lime juice (2 medium limes)

3 tablespoons extra virgin olive oil

3 tablespoons unsalted butter, melted

3 tablespoons chopped fresh cilantro leaves

1 tablespoon pure red chile powder

1/4 teaspoon cayenne

Salt to taste

1 red bell pepper

1 yellow bell pepper

1 poblano chile

1 zucchini, cut on a bias into 1/2-inch-thick rounds

1 yellow squash, cut on a bias into 1/2-inch-thick rounds

1 large red onion, cut into 1/2-inch-thick rounds

2 ears sweet corn, shucked and each cut crosswise into 4 rounds

1 large eggplant, cut into 1-inch-thick rounds

2 large portobello mushrooms, quartered

To prepare the aïoli, whisk together the mayonnaise, garlic, and lemon zest. Keep refrigerated.

To prepare the vegetables, place the lime juice, oil, butter, cilantro, chile powder, cayenne, and salt in a mixing bowl and whisk to combine. Seed and quarter lengthwise the bell peppers and poblano. In a separate large mixing bowl, place the peppers, poblano, zucchini, yellow squash, onion, corn, eggplant, and mushrooms. Add the lime juice mixture and toss carefully to coat all the vegetables.

Grill the tossed vegetables over direct medium-high heat for 6 to 10 minutes, or until tender, turning once or twice. Season with additional salt as the vegetables come off the grill, if desired. Serve on a large platter; drizzle the vegetables with the aïoli, or serve it as a dip. SERVES: 4

The deep purple, lusciously plump Mission figs are so-called because Spanish Franciscan missionaries brought them to the New World. They are in season late June to October—prime grilling season! To save time, substitute your favorite store-bought ice cream.

Figs from the Grill
with Ginger Ice Cream

To prepare the figs, place the honey, Marsala, and vanilla in a bowl and stir together to combine. Add the figs and marinate for 2 hours.

To prepare the ice cream, blanch the ginger in boiling water for 30 seconds and drain well. Place the egg yolks, sugar, and salt in a mixing bowl and whisk until thick, creamy, and light in color. Place the blanched ginger, cream, vanilla extract, and corn syrup in a saucepan. Bring to a boil, reduce heat, and simmer for 5 minutes to let the flavors infuse. Strain into a clean saucepan and reheat. Vigorously stir ½ cup of this mixture into the egg mixture to temper the eggs, then add the tempered egg mixture to the saucepan. Reduce the heat to medium and cook, stirring constantly, until the mixture is thick enough to coat the back of a spoon. Do not let boil or overcook. Strain into a stainless steel bowl and cool over ice water. Transfer to an ice cream machine and freeze according to the manufacturer's directions (about 30 minutes).

Remove the figs from the marinade, drain any excess liquid, and set aside. Pour the marinade into a saucepan. Bring to a boil, reduce heat, and simmer until ½ cup remains, about 8 to 10 minutes. Grill the figs over direct medium heat for 2 to 3 minutes per side. Spoon 1 or 2 tablespoons of the warm marinade onto serving plates and arrange 2 figs on top of the sauce on each plate. Serve with the ice cream.

SERVES: 4

FIGS
- ½ cup honey
- ½ cup Marsala or port wine
- 1 teaspoon vanilla extract
- 8 fresh figs (preferably Mission)

ICE CREAM
- 1 cup peeled and very finely minced fresh ginger
- 4 large egg yolks
- ½ cup sugar
- Pinch of salt
- 1¾ cups heavy cream
- 1 teaspoon vanilla extract
- ¼ cup corn syrup

Here is proof that grilling fruit can be remarkably successful. Stilton and port are classic accompaniments to pears. Substitute other pear varieties (or apples) and your favorite blue cheese. The port sauce is less viscous when cool, but serve warm if you prefer.

Grilled
Sweet Pears
with Stilton & Port Sauce

SAUCE

3 cups port

1/4 teaspoon crushed black peppercorns

4 cloves

PEARS

2 Bartlett or Anjou pears

2 tablespoons freshly squeezed lemon juice (1 small lemon)

2 teaspoons sugar

1/4 cup crumbled Stilton blue cheese

To prepare the sauce, pour the port into a saucepan, add the peppercorns and cloves, and bring to a boil. Turn down the heat and simmer until reduced to 1/2 cup, 30 to 40 minutes. Strain and let cool.

Peel the pears, cut in half lengthwise, and core with a melon baller or paring knife. Place on a plate and sprinkle with the lemon juice and sugar, making sure both sides are moistened. Grill the pears, cut-side down, over direct medium heat for 3 or 4 minutes. Turn and grill 3 minutes longer, or until tender. Cut a thin slice off the bottom of each pear so that they will sit evenly on the plate.

Spoon the sauce onto each serving plate. Place a pear half, cut-side up, on the edge of each pool of sauce. Arrange the cheese inside the pear cavities and sprinkle extra around the plate, if desired.

SERVES: 4

Finger bananas, also sold as apple bananas, have a wonderfully sweet and full flavor and are the perfect size for this recipe. Sabayon (zabaglione in Italy) is the supremely light, custard-like French classic. Use it as soon as possible; it doesn't keep well.

Seared
Finger Bananas
with Creamy Cointreau Sabayon

SABAYON

2 large egg yolks

3 tablespoons sugar

1/4 cup Cointreau

1/4 cup heavy cream

BANANAS

1/4 cup freshly squeezed orange juice (1 small orange)

3 tablespoons dark rum

2 tablespoons brown sugar

Pinch of salt

3 tablespoons butter

8 sweet finger bananas, or 4 regular bananas, unpeeled

To prepare the sabayon, combine the egg yolks and sugar in a mixing bowl. Stir in the Cointreau and transfer to a double boiler over high heat. Vigorously whisk the mixture for 5 or 6 minutes until soft peaks form and the mixture doubles or triples in volume. Remove from the heat and place over a bowl of ice water. Continue whisking until completely chilled. Using an electric mixer, whisk the cream at high speed until soft peaks form. Gently fold into the egg mixture until thoroughly combined. Keep refrigerated until ready to serve.

To prepare the bananas, place the orange juice, rum, sugar, and salt in a saucepan and stir over medium heat until the sugar is dissolved. Bring to a boil and reduce by half, about 4 or 5 minutes. Stir in the butter until melted and remove from the heat. Cut the bananas in half lengthwise, keeping the peel on. Brush the banana flesh liberally with the sauce and grill flesh-side down over direct medium heat for 2 or 3 minutes, or until seared. Turn over, brush again, and grill for 2 minutes. Spoon 2 tablespoons of the remaining warm sauce on each plate. Remove the bananas from the peel; if using regular bananas, cut in half crosswise. Arrange the bananas on the sauce and top with the sabayon.

SERVES: 4

Appendix A:
Basic Recipes

Grilled Garlic

Grilling garlic helps to mellow the bitter edge of raw garlic and makes it sweeter. It also softens it so there is no need to purée it. Garlic can be grilled while other foods are also "receiving the treatment." Rub whole heads of garlic with olive oil and place on the edge of direct medium heat (or over indirect medium to medium-high heat). Grill for about 40 to 45 minutes, turning every 10 minutes, until the outer skin is brown but not burned. The cloves should be soft, and you should be able to squeeze the roasted garlic out of each clove once you have snipped off the top.

Grilled Bell Peppers and Chiles

Grilling bell peppers and chiles not only gives them smoky, sweet, and sometimes complex flavors, but it is also the best way to prepare them for peeling.

Grill whole peppers or chiles (with stems attached) over direct medium-high heat, turning frequently until blackened all over, about 10 to 15 minutes; do not overcook or you will scorch or burn the flesh. Remove with tongs and place in a metal bowl. Cover with plastic wrap and let "steam" for 10 minutes.

When cool enough to handle, peel off the skin with your fingers or with the tip of a sharp knife. Avoid peeling roasted peppers and chiles under water—the natural oils and flavor will be diminished.

Split the peppers or chiles open with a knife and remove the stem, seeds, and internal ribs.

Bell peppers and chiles can be roasted ahead of time and kept in the refrigerator for 2 or 3 days. They can also be frozen.

Puréed Chiles

In this book we call mostly for puréed canned chipotle chiles. These are dried smoked jalapeños that are canned with a spicy adobo broth. Simply place some of the chiles, with the broth, in a blender or food processor, and purée. It is worth puréeing a batch and keeping it in an airtight container in the refrigerator.

For other dried chiles, use the procedure for rehydrating ancho chiles described on page 86. Drain and purée, adding a little of the rehydrating liquid if needed to make puréeing possible.

Blanched Tomatoes

Blanching tomatoes makes them easy to peel while keeping the texture intact. Bring a saucepan of water to a boil. Score the base of the tomatoes with an x and immerse in the boiling water for 30 seconds. Remove with a slotted spoon and transfer to an ice bath to stop the cooking process. Peel with the tip of a sharp knife, starting at the base end.

"Time hath a taming hand."
John Henry Cardinal Newman

Appendix B:
Cooking Times

Cooking times depend on innumerable factors, including the size of the fire and the heat of the grill, the distance of the cooking grate from the heat source, the size, thickness, and temperature of the meat or ingredient being grilled, altitude, and weather conditions, to name a few. The cooking times given in the preceding recipes should therefore be considered guidelines, rather than hard-and-fast rules; be prepared to be flexible.

While the traditional rules about allowing so much time per pound are helpful, the most reliable method of knowing when food is cooked to your liking is to use a meat thermometer (see page 19). The chart below of internal temperature for each stage of doneness reflects *fully cooked* temperatures, allowing for a few minutes of standing time to let the meat juices redistribute internally for best results (this does not apply to cuts less than 1 inch thick). Therefore, at the time you remove meat from the grill, internal temperature should be 5˚F to 10˚F lower than those listed because residual heat will cause the temperature of the meat to continue rising after it has been removed from the heat source. We have not included temperatures for well-done meat, as we discourage overcooking; however, you can allow 5˚F to 10˚F more than medium-well, if you insist on incineration!

Check for doneness often, using a meat thermometer, or develop your skill at testing meat with your finger, a skill you can practice every few minutes as the meat cooks. Rare meat will feel soft; medium-rare will feel somewhat soft but have some firmness on the outside; at medium, it will have a springy firmness. Well-done meat will feel very firm and unyielding. If need be, test doneness by using a knife to pierce the meat; err on the side of checking this before it's too late.

Internal Temperatures (Ready to Eat)

	Rare	Medium-Rare	Medium	Medium-Well
Beef	130	140	150	165
Pork	•	•	160	165-170
Lamb	130	140	150	165
Poultry	•	•	•	175
Fowl	•	150	160	170
Seafood	•	150	160	170

• *Where no figures are given, consumption is not recommended. Note that USDA recommendations are 5˚F to 10˚F higher at each stage of cooking than the temperatures listed here, primarily because of food-safety concerns. If you wish to err on the side of caution, bear this in mind. The internal temperature at which all meat bacteria are killed is 160˚F, although poultry should be cooked to at least 175˚F*

Cooking Times

The approximate cooking times that follow assume direct grilling over medium-high to high heat unless otherwise noted. For those items listed as cooked over indirect heat, this assumes the grill is covered.

In the preceding recipes, we specified grilling for the same amount of time on each side. However, if you prefer, cook a little longer on the first side (for example, if the total cooking time is 10 to 12 minutes, grill 6 to 7 minutes on the first side, and 4 to 5 on the second); the second side will be warming even while it is away from the direct heat. Unless otherwise specified in the recipes, it is best to turn smaller cuts of meat (including steaks and chops) just once.

Pork	Thickness/Weight	Time (total minutes for both sides)	
		M-Rare	Medium
4 oz. chops	1 inch	NR	8 to 10
8 oz. chops	1 inch	NR	10 to 12
Loin*	12 oz.	NR	25 to 30
Spare ribs*	1½ lbs. rack	NR	60 to 75
Baby back ribs*	1½ lbs. rack	NR	70 to 80

NR: *not recommended* * *grilled over indirect medium heat*

Beef	Thickness/ Weight	Time (total minutes for both sides)	
		M-Rare	Medium
8 oz. hamburger	3/4 inch	NR	10 to 12*
6 oz. rib-eye	3/4 inch	5 to 6	7 to 8
7 oz. sirloin	1 inch	8 to 9	10 to 12
1 lb. porterhouse	1 inch	10 to 11	12 to 14
7 oz. filet mignon	1½ inches	10 to 11	12 to 14
Flank steak	1½ lbs.	10 to 12	14 to 16
Rib-eye roast**	4 lbs.	60 to 90	90 to 120

NR: *not recommended* * *until internal temperature reaches 160˚F*
** *grilled over indirect medium heat*

Lamb	Thickness/ Weight	Time (total minutes for both sides)	
		M-Rare	Medium
8 oz. steaks	3/4 inch	6 to 7	8 to 10
6 oz. rib chops	1¾ inches	11 to 12	14 to 16
Rack*	2 lbs.	35 to 40	40 to 45
Leg, boneless*	4 lbs.	45 to 50	55 to 60
Leg, bone-in*	6 lbs.	110 to 120	135

* *grilled over indirect medium heat*

Chicken	Thickness/ Weight	Time (total minutes for both sides)
		Done
Boneless breast	4 oz.	10 to 12
Wings		12 to 15
Whole*	3 lbs.	75 to 80
Whole*	4 lbs.	90 to 95

* *grilled over indirect medium heat*

Turkey	Thickness/ Weight	Time (total minutes for both sides)
Whole*	12 lbs.	About 3 hours

* *grilled over indirect medium heat*

Duck	Thickness/Weight	Time (total minutes for both sides)
Whole*	5 lbs.	About 2 hours

* *grilled over indirect medium heat*

Seafood	Thickness/Weight	Time (total minutes for both sides)
		Medium
Fish filets	½ inch	5 to 7
Fish filets	1 inch	8 to 10
Fish steaks	1 inch	9 to 12
Whole fish*	2 lbs.	25 to 30
Lobster tails	6 oz.	12 to 15
Scallops	Sea	2 to 5
Shrimp	Jumbo	4 to 6

* *grilled over indirect medium heat*

Vegetables	Thickness/Weight	Time (total minutes for both sides)
Asparagus	Thin/thick	3 to 4 / 6 to 8
Corn	Whole ear	8 to 10
Corn*	Whole ear	12 to 15
Eggplant	Sliced	12 to 15
Mushrooms	Domestic	7 to 8
Mushrooms	Portobello	10 to 12
Onions	Sliced	6 to 8
Bell peppers	Whole	12 to 15 (charred)
Squash	Sliced	8 to 10
Tomatoes	Whole	10 to 12 (charred)

* *grilled over indirect medium heat*

Appendix C:
Resources

Steaks and Meat

Omaha Steaks
11030 O Street, Omaha, NE 68137
To order: (800) 228-9055
Customer Service: (800) 228-9872
www.omahasteaks.com

Grills, Smokers, and Accessories

Barbecues Galore
15041 Bake Parkway, Suite A, Irvine, CA 92618
(800) GRILL-UP (474-5587)
www.bbqgalore.com

Char-Broil
P.O. Box 1240, Columbus, GA 31902
(800) 241-7548
www.charbroil.com

Chef's Catalog
P.O. Box 620048, Dallas, TX 75262-0048
(800) 338-3232
www.chefscatalog.com

Ducane Gas Grills, Inc.
800 Dutch Square Boulevard, Columbia, SC 29210
(803) 798-1600
www.ducane.com

Viking Range Corporation
P.O. Box 956, Greenwood, MS 38935
(662) 455-1200
www.vikingrange.com

Weber-Stephen Products Company
200 East Daniels Road, Palatine, IL 60067-6266
(800) 446-1071
www.weberbbq.com

Charcoal and Smoking Woods

Charcoal Companion
7955 Edgewater Drive, Oakland, CA 94621
(800) 521-0505
www.charcoalcompanion.com

Lazzari Fuel Company
P.O. Box 34051, San Francisco, CA 94134
(800) 242-7265
www.lazzarifuelcompany.com

Kitchen Equipment, Accessories (Including Grills, Smokers, and Tableware), and Ingredients

Baker's Catalogue (spices, flours, & grains)
P.O. Box 876, Norwich, VT 05055
(800) 827-6836
www.kingarthurflour.com

Crate & Barrel
P.O. Box 3210, Naperville, IL 60566
(800) 323-5461
www.crateandbarrel.com

Melissa's World Variety Produce, Inc.
P.O. Box 21127, Los Angeles, CA 90021
(800) 588-0151
www.melissas.com

Williams-Sonoma
P.O. Box 379900, Las Vegas, NV 89137
(800) 541-2233
www.williams-sonoma.com

Information about Meat Nutrition, Food Safety, and Industry Practices

American Meat Institute
Public Affairs Department
P.O. Box 3556
Washington, D.C. 20007
(703) 841-2400
www.meatami.org

Beef and Veal Culinary Center
National Cattlemen's Beef Association
5420 South Quebec Street
Greenwood Village, CO 80111
(800) 525-3085
www.beef.org

Acknowledgments

I am very thankful for the help of many colleagues and employees at Omaha Steaks. My son, Todd, served as my business and marketing partner as before. Dave Hershiser, our chief financial officer, was a big help with the business details. Bob Bezousek, our director of plant operations, supervised the preparation and shipping of all the Omaha Steaks products for recipe preparation, testing, and photography. Greg Smolen, a superb journeyman meat cutter, prepared all the cuts to exact specifications. Jackie Thompson, our staff home economist, read the manuscript and offered helpful suggestions. Thanks in advance to Jim Paschal, our director of marketing, and our public relations team, Sharon Bargas and Lynn Kampschneider, for organizing and executing the marketing and promotion of the book, and communicating many details between authors and publisher. Deb Righter, my secretary, handled all of my contacts in a timely and professional way.

— F. S.

First, my thanks to my wife, Trez, who served valiantly as guinea pig, sounding board, and recipe consultant. Next, accolades to Terry Finlayson, my colleague who tested many of the recipes in this book. As always, her expertise, professionalism, and good taste are highly valued.

Fred joins me in thanking Tim Turner's photographic "Dream Team" in Chicago: Lynn Gagné, one of the best food stylists anywhere; Renée Miller, an innovative and inspirational prop stylist; Cindy Melin, Lynn's talented assistant; Rod (Mr. Jeep) La Fleur, witty, helpful, and hardworking assistant to Tim; Bart Witowski, Tim's other invaluable assistant; and Tiffany Butler, studio manager, and a good reason why the Turner Studio hums along so efficiently. And above all, our gratitude to Tim, whose extraordinary artistic and technical skills (as well as his knowledgeable recipe suggestions and advice) make him the consummate food photographer. Lads and lasses, it was fun for us and we hope it was for you too!

And last, but by no means least, our friends at Clarkson Potter: Katie Workman, senior editor, who believed in this project and in us; Chris Pavone for his skillful and insightful editing; and Julia Coblentz, for her invaluable assistance and project coordination.

— J. H.

Index